ENLIGHTENMENT OF MIND

Lankavatara Mindfulness

by

Karna Sonam Tarjay

ISBN ebook# 979-8-9902473-1-4

Table of Contents

Introduction

Prepare to embark on a transformative journey. This book doesn't gently guide you; it immerses you in profound insights beyond the norm. **These are the words of the Buddha, refreshed and linked to modern scientific theories and contemporary life.** If you find them challenging, embrace the surprise of learning.

At its core, *Enlightenment of Mind* empowers you to manifest the life you desire through several understandings.

We know the importance of pausing, listening, and being present in difficult times, finding enlightenment in a simple breath or a quiet moment of stillness. But what about our dreams, seemingly unsolvable problems, or the everyday challenges of being human? Here, the magic lies, akin to the slow, deliberate growth of a mighty oak from a tiny acorn.

Imagine setting a problem, vision, or idea firmly in your mind, then releasing your attachment to specific outcomes. By letting go, you create space for an inspirational connection with the subconscious field of creativity and wisdom. Suddenly, unexpected ideas bloom, solutions emerge, relationships flourish, and synchronicities abound.

This is where the true magic happens, where the seemingly impossible becomes possible, and where the ordinary transforms into the extraordinary. **This book invites you to explore every aspect of your life with a new paradigm of understanding.**

The transliterations in this book are the culmination of studying the *Lankavatara Sutra (Lanka)* as translated by D.T. Suzuki and the prose it inspired. The *Lanka* stands out among the ancient texts emerging from Indian Sanskrit roots, a lineage shared by only a handful of sutras. Unlike the *Diamond*

Sutra or the *Heart Sutra*, which gained widespread recognition and acceptance, the *Lanka* remained enigmatic, veiled in mystery, and translations other than D.T. Suzuki's often omitted a significant portion of the original text.

So, what makes the *Lanka* so unique? While other sutras found social acceptability, **the *Lanka* dared to challenge the foundations of societal norms, religion, and governance. This defiance included the abhorrence of slavery, class systems, superstitious beliefs, and the divinity of those in power.** The *Lanka* demanded more than what the established powers were willing to concede. The *Lanka's* radical ideas were considered too provocative, disruptive, and dangerous to the status quo.

The *Lanka* delves into the depths of consciousness, presenting a vision of reality that defies conventional understanding. It speaks of Mind-only, suchness, and freedom from the outcomes of thought, concepts that encourage introspection of one's place in the universe.

However, such profound insights came at a cost. The transformative potential of the *Lanka* was seen as a threat by those in power. **Its teachings implied a liberation that extended beyond personal enlightenment to societal responsibility, questioning the very foundations of authority and control.** As a result, it was relegated to the dusty shelves, its wisdom hidden from the mainstream.

In my previous books I provided references and frameworks from physics, biology, and psychology to support the *Lanka's* unique paradigm. These disciplines offer a modern lens through which we can appreciate the insights of this ancient text.

What treasures remain hidden on that dusty shelf? What wisdom has been overlooked, waiting to be rediscovered by those willing to delve into the depths of the *Lanka*?

The *Lanka's* thesis is that all suffering and worldly ills stem from the delusion of separateness. Its paradigm includes understanding our natural assets and limitations. Most importantly, this book presents a fantastic psychology of conscious evolution.

"Enlightenment of Mind" does not focus on the religious aspects of Buddhism, except where they illuminate human potential. Like my best poem, it is more about being, than doing or collecting.

Secret Koans, OWM

I see what I want to see, I hear what I want to hear, accountable for interpretation, and creation, I am.

My undisciplined mind views reality through reruns of experience, habitual thinking calls a self-fulfilling prophecy.

Thinking habits must change, past emotions must corrupt My present perception no more. Not controlled or offended, I see you, eye to eye.

No one other than self is ever responsible.

Hobbling fear, wondering desire, or discipline understood, **All thought is prayer, all prayer is answered.**

I call my soul's desire in quiet moments. I call other things unaware.

Demonstration lifts me, grace detonates my self-will, consuming reservation.

Faith is to do, not just believe.

Our fathers blamed desire, following that, I've made myself a hypocrite. Better to be honestly flawed, as desire always finds a way.

In error, I've grown also, to desire less naturally; falling away as they seem.

Selfish desires mature, exchanged, replaced with selfless desire. Higher for

6

lower, mind is the choice and the work. **Desire is the vehicle and source. commencement of creation, God desires us.**

Truth spoken is not the whole truth. Truth is a place beyond my mind, where I cannot be right if it makes you wrong.

Love described is hardly its shadow; relationships invent each moment. If we are both in this place, there is only one of us here. In love, there is no other than self.

Joy misunderstood at root, the only gift I have for you, me. **Joy, more than my right, is my purpose and my duty.** Finding my own joys gift, I have something to offer you.

I see what I want to see; I hear what I want to hear.

In this book, I use terms that may initially seem metaphoric. Concepts like the subconscious, entanglement, and the field of life interdependently co-arising are pivotal to my understanding of the Sutra and its connection to modern physics, psychology, and biology. **These are not just abstract ideas; they relate directly to Quantum Physics, the Observer Effect, Quantum Entanglement, Morphogenetic Field Theory, and related Microbiology, as elaborated in "Seven Stages of Consciousness."**

This approach diverges from classical Buddhism and mainstream science to present the *Lanka's* thesis of a non-separate reality. Imagine the thrill of uncovering how ancient wisdom aligns with cutting-edge scientific discoveries, revealing the interconnectedness of all life.

Embrace the adventure where the wisdom of the past and the revelations of the present converge to illuminate the path to your highest potential.

CHAPTER ONE
Listening and Human Suffering

The first Chapter from the *Lankavatara Sutra* begins with the sudden awakening of Ravana, Lord of Lanka. He represents our natural sense consciousness and the myriad aspects of our lower nature. As such, he is also the lord of all worldly knowledge, especially beliefs, opinions, and judgment. But he also represents our playful selves not to be discounted. **In the following section, guidance on listening highlights the transformative potential of mindful awareness.**

The chapter opens with a powerful and joyous vision of the Buddha, whose laughter and wisdom capture the attention of divine beings. The Buddha addresses Ravana, emphasizing the critical role of open and intuitive listening in spiritual growth. He advises Ravana to set aside distractions and preconceived notions, urging him to listen with his entire being, to access deeper wisdom in the clear view of his own reactions.

Lanka: Chapter 1

The Buddha's eye of wisdom warmed with joy. Then a knowing smile emerged like the most glorious sunrise. ***The Awakened Self (Buddha) then roared a deafening laugh that rivaled anything ever heard in all the realms of heaven or earth.*** *His body blazed with the light of a newborn sun at the beginning of an age. The Gods and Guardians of Creation took notice, and with the Bodhisattvas, they were shocked, surprised, and concerned....*

Buddha addressed their questions and concerns, "My amusement and roaring laughter were in anticipation of Ravana's next question. Ravana, your presence in this spiritual journey is not just significant, it is crucial. You hold a unique place in this journey, and your questions are not just permitted, they are encouraged. **However, remember, your role is not just to ask, but to listen with an open, uncluttered mind.** *Look within your heart, and I will be there to satisfy your need.*

Concentrated listening is not just a requirement, it is a gateway to your greatest lessons. **Your journey will be enriched by the awareness of your reactions.** *Recognize your distracting thoughts and emotions, but do not let them control you.* **Listen intently, setting everything aside so you may understand what is presented, as your own wisdom arising.**

Rest in tranquil understanding and let go of preconceptions. Be unbound from self-limiting reactions and free of judgment and opinions. **See the highest truth within yourself by intuitive open listening.** *Finding oneness is not a daunting task, it is a journey of acceptance of all, where no one is greater, no one is lesser.*

Intuition beyond imagination will reveal the field of being as your subconscious self. It begins in accepting awareness. **Set yourself to listening with your entire being and awakening will be yours.**
Don't confuse this with the enlightenment of the conscious mind; this is Mind-only."

Mind-only is *Lanka's* cornerstone. **It means we create an experiential reality based on our preferences, beliefs, and judgments.**

Lanka: Chapter 3, section LVIII

What is the source or mother of sentient beings?

Desire procreates, as a mixture of joy and anger, but nurtured through motherly instinct.

9

Ignorance provides the seed, to guide his children into the realms of pleasure and suffering.

However humble our beginnings, ***it is only through mastering our animal natures and its delusion, that we may attain freedom and our true potential.***

The *Lanka* highlights the problem and opportunity that most of us are caught in habitual thinking that controls our experience of reality. Are you only your thoughts? Without labels, who are you?

The following section looks at human challenges in the three worlds of form, desire, and thought (formlessness).

Lanka: **Chapter 1,**

Buddha whispered, "Ravana, people are paralyzed in life experience, trapped by habitual likes and dislikes. ***Their turmoil grows from infatuation with experience to dissatisfaction, at the whim of who they think they are.*** *Isn't it apparent? Why do so few recognize their self-imposed suffering?*

All beliefs and prejudice evolved based on similar habitual ideas, but they only lead to naïve, relative truths and untruths. ***Sadly, this is beyond most people, as they are oblivious or unaware of nature's inherent limitations.*** *It leaves them insecure to let go their story and accept themselves as beyond names and forms.*

Beyond the normality of sleepwalking through life, is a self-realization of one's essential worth, not limited to self-image but available through transmission (Dharma). This Noble Wisdom is beyond mere words but not to consider it, is a tragedy.

Many well-meaning people worry for those others that only believe in what they can see and measure. But this is the natural state of sense consciousness, which we all go through. **The wise recognize limiting oneself to physical reality through their own experience as the behavior of children."**

Lanka: **Chapter 3, Section LXXVII**

False notions are those which misjudge things as other than they are. Reality is mistaken through clinging to the idea of a separate existence, wherein actuality is distorted by our perception.

For this reason, intuitive penetration converts mere knowledge to wisdom. Free from bitter cycles of struggle, it means release from discrimination and the loosening of conviction. Beliefs can be seen as temporary, maybe useful, but unworthy of much defence.

When everything is seen, as the construction of the mind, offended responses cease and one may consider what effortlessness means.

Can you see yourself reacting without thinking? How much of life have you missed out on because things remind you of something you did not like in the past?

The Buddha illuminates a path of liberation, available through intuitively transcending mere knowledge. **In this way overcoming habitual reactions and judgments, you can attain a profound, effortless understanding of life.** This journey invites you to recognize all experiences as constructs of the mind, empowering your freedom to embrace a life of deeper clarity and peace. This story leads to understanding what liberation and awakening truly mean.

CHAPTER TWO
Mind-only

This chapter delves into the concept of "Mind-only", a cornerstone of Buddhist philosophy that transcends psychological understanding. You're invited to see suffering as a doorway to effortless being, where compulsions and false imaginations burn away. In this state, we transcend childishness, seeing the world as it truly is without projections.

Your Creation, OWM

In the quiet depths where silence reigns, effortless being, the soul unchains. Preference and prejudice dissolve like mist, thoughts and wants no longer insist.

Life's lessons, a sacred syllabus, repeated till suffering meets its hush. Through this portal, grace unfolds, compulsion burns, and imagination molds.

In connection's embrace, a symphony plays, listening, joy, love, in endless arrays. Here and now, in pure suchness dwell, childishness fades, in wisdom's well.

The world unfolds, its truth revealed, no projections veil, all is healed. Mind's power harnessed, understood with grace, thou art beyond, in boundless space.

Not the mind's confines, but spirit's flight, In the quiet, where truth shines bright. **In this moment's peace, find your truest hue, in the depth of being, where skies renew.**

Lanka: **D.T. SUZUKI, Ontology an Twofold Egolessness**

The theory of Mind-only (Cittamatra) cannot be fully grasped in psychological terms because Citta does not mean only our individual mind. As the absolute mind, Mind-only takes awareness and creation beyond thinking and imagination. It is a state of awareness understood to perceive the highest reality.

The highest reality says, everything is perfect just as it is, but we can not see it in our delusion. *However, enlightened beings experience life effortlessly, where worldly chaos is seen compassionately as a necessary part of each persons conscious evolution.*

Some people, look for and progressively experience this perfection, embracing synchronicities and living each moment in joy, which shapes a personality of loving kindness. This is their service, to live fully present, fully listening in seeking the enlightened view.

The highest reality is also known as suchness; truth and authenticity as the state of naked awareness, creating an environment of acceptance.

But truth is beyond interpretation, life only emerges all together. Everything is interdependently co-arising with no one in judgment of its evolution.

Lanka: D.T. Suzuki, Chapter 2, section IX,

*The meditative consciousness of suchness, and the correct acquisition of truth can be understood as equivalent, because **they refer to a singularity of mind, concentrated and focused thought, in the receptive state of intuition, rather than the active state of thinking.***

This idea of focused singularity as concentrated intuition is another way of describing suchness. Do you notice how helpful it is just to stop when things get confusing or emotional? When we're really interested in something or someone, **we listen with every fiber of our being. That is suchness, the natural state of your quiet focused mind.**

Grace, OWM

Alone with God, in whispered embrace, I seek His message, in every place. Life mirrors mind, in mentor's sway, if I could but see, all's infinite day.

We are one, in infinite's embrace, teardrops to ocean's boundless grace.

Your expression, his voice untold, purified to hear, as truths unfold.

Earth, our greater self, continents breathe, corpuscles in harmony, life's grand weave. Chaos a myth, in design we find, synchronicity's the dance, through joy entwined.

Supernatural real, corporeal mere, relationships craft each moment dear.

In knowing this place, one truth rings clear, here and now, who you are, sincere.

Mind-only and suchness are just names for mindfulness. **Suchness is the clearing of mind stuff as the tool to appreciate we are all just making it up as we go along.** Do you ever notice how the whole world seems happy when you are? Have you ever noticed how the world is just as disturbed as you allow?

Chapter Two concludes that Mind-only and suchness guide us to embrace our responsibility in reacting to life's challenges. With a quiet, intuitive mind, you can perceive the highest reality of impermanent ever changing life, by seeing perfection in everything as it is. **As we clear our minds and embrace the suchness of listening, we uncover the inherent joy in every moment, shaping a life of loving-kindness and synchronicity.**

CHAPTER THREE
Nirvana

Welcome to the exploration of Nirvana. Here, we challenge common misconceptions to understand Nirvana not as an escape from suffering but as a radical shift in awareness, transcending the duality of pain and pleasure.

Lanka: Chapter 2, section XVIII

Some people think emotion is suffering, rather than a choice of response. While still afraid of life and death sufferings, they seek nirvana as freedom from pain, not realizing the inseparability of suffering and nirvana in all things subject to thinking. ***They imagine renouncing senses and desires, not realizing that nirvana is a radical shift in awareness altering one's subconscious fabric.***

Thinking is only useful to see one's self-delusion and compulsive habits. The problem is not desire or the senses, it is identification of self as thought, preferences etc. ***The subconscious transformation begins with a partial sudden awakening, but self-realization, and the Great Turning Back are changes at one's core.***

Lanka: Chapter 2, section LXXIV

*Painful consequences and turmoil, lead some people to understand that belief and identification with the world is the cause of suffering. Not understanding that all belief, identification, and experience is only the creation of mind, they seek nirvana. But a good belief isn't much better than a bad one. Because**, all views of nirvana are flawed where they depend on understanding**.*

16

Nirvana is an awareness of the non-dual where there is no subject, object, or cause and effect. Without delusion in nirvana, there is nothing rising, nothing falling and no place for belief.

So, in identification with habitual thinking, no matter what the intentions, one may only wander around confused that nirvana is not found anywhere.

slokas

75. *When perception is not understood to be a mental construction, compulsive habit dictates life. If understood, one ceases to sleep walk, remaining fully present to what is.*

76. ***Here the mind finds freedom, undisturbed even by accomplishment or ambition. In this awareness all things are perceived clearly, just as they are.***

Lanka: **Chapter 3, Section LXVIII**

Humankind clings to and craves the positive signs of doing good, without realizing it often mirrors separation and insult. *Even in achieving a higher purpose, we often devalue another's path because it looks different to our own.* ***Not yet seeing the perfection within other lives, we fail to understand it is beyond our discrimination.***

Those of highest intention awaken to understand the inconsequential nature of labels, especially when they hide distinctions of higher and lower. ***The essential meaning of awakening self, is to recognize the awakening in everyone.***

This may be the most difficult paradigm shift for the Western mind, grasping what it means to be awake per the *Lanka*. **Awakening first recognizes our self-delusion in what we think, who we think we are, and the illusion that outcomes of thought are truth.**

Free Will, OWM

Free, free at last, beyond mere whim, thou art unbound from mind's dark brim. **No bondage holds, in each moment's grace, from compulsion's grip, find freedom's embrace.**

Truth of being, in emptiness's core, unchanging knowledge, for evermore. No need to grasp, control unwinds, prejudice fades, as freedom finds.

Past shadows fade, habits relent, discrimination's hold, now spent. **Solitude between thoughts, serene and pure, in emptiness, oneness, all things endure.**

Collecting, doing, being whole, letting go of outcomes, freedom's goal. No beliefs restrain, no doubts persist, selfless ambition, with intention kissed.

Acceptance blooms, in moments still, what is, is freedom's gentle will. False imaginations with preferences fade, openness to joy, in love's cavalcade.

Thou art free, as purpose guides, in openness, where freedom truly abides.

Lanka: Chapter 2, Section XX

Five avenues of spiritual insight were understood in ancient times. They include renunciation of ignorance, following enlightened beings from other paths, and realizing the not-separate nature of all things, just as they are. Additionally, there are unknown groups of indefinite character; and those to whom insight is not relevant, maybe impossible.

The renunciates of ignorance respond to insight with joy to understand through appearances. So, their body hair might stand on end as they grasp the five aspects of sentient beings, the seven first self-natures, or the eight channels of consciousness because it allows the understanding of this existence. *But this path is to do away with the rising of passions without addressing the habitual compulsions of mental identification* Through this means of renouncing ignorance one may eventually find oneness, nirvana and even Buddhahood. But the final step, will mean they must progress beyond the habitual identification with thought.

There are also those who follow Buddhas of other paths. Their truth response to spiritual insight is broader, through understanding, synchronicity, and also the interdependent co-arising of all things. When feeling the insights of solitude, selflessness, and worldly detachment, they may shed tears, or the hair of their body may stand on end. These followers of other paths, may also develop powers of transformation , meditative consciousness and Buddhahood, to the extent they are true to their path. Conformity to their own traditions and stepping beyond the outcomes of thought will gauge progress.

For followers of Buddhist tradition there are three predominant aspects or paths of spiritual insight. *First is realizing the not-separate nature of all things, just as they are. Second is the insight of self-realization (not two, no other than self). Third is the devotion of insight into the transcendental field of being, Buddha-lands.* These insights arise from the variety of traditions to transform the realm of subconscious knowledge

Spiritual insight for unknown groups of indefinite character are according to the same natural laws but they differ in understanding, and cultural diversity. *However, life's great teachings are no less available and*

sudden awakening may arise in a myriad of ways to anyone. It is often recognized as terrible misfortune but everyone experiences the collection of experience, things, opinions and beliefs, only to see them become of no value in old age. The same is true of those to whom spiritual insight is irrelevant. **The world may change in an instant but often the greatest lesson is tragedy.**

The five avenues of spiritual insight provide a glimpse into the ancient worldview that existed on the Indian subcontinent almost two thousand years ago. This perspective, while rooted in a specific time and place, can still resonate with us today, even if we find ourselves in groups of indefinite character or following Buddhas of other paths. **The underlying message remains clear, life is our most profound teacher, and awakening is a subtle shift in perspective**.

Can you identify the key to this awakening in observing your habitual reactions, limiting beliefs, and ways of thinking?

Chapter Three illuminated the path to Nirvana by letting go of the outcomes and recognizing the interconnectedness of all things. Also, **this journey, rather than renouncing desires or seeking escape, is about penetrating one's subconscious authenticity and embracing the present moment with clarity and compassion.** Deconstructing habitual reactions and limiting beliefs is difficult at best. So, the process or method is to make progress in reprograming life with constructs of non-reaction and exercises of acceptance.

CHAPTER FOUR
Stages of Consciousness

Embark on this unique journey that unveils stages of consciousness or self-natures range from the collection of material things to the realization of Buddha nature. **They reveal the transformative potential within each of us.** Let curiosity guide you as we uncover the mysteries of consciousness and their significance in our lives.

Understanding these seven self-natures was unique for me, through the transliteration of the *Lanka*.

Lanka: **Chapter 2, Section V**

*There are seven stages of conscious awareness or kinds of self-nature, which culminate in oneness and effortless belonging. (1) **Collection** of things, experience and status for self, narcissism, (2) **Belonging** and devotion as in family and tribal relationships, (3) Characteristic marks of **not belonging** to the compulsive, normal lifestyle, (4) Formless **spiritual consciousness**, (5) Objective wisdom to observe causal forces, **non-dual rationality**, (6) **Certitude** through experience of life's interdependence and conditionality, suchness, oneness, and nirvana, (7) **Perfect awareness**, Buddha nature realized.*

The journey ranges from selfish awareness to understanding and experiencing natural law (the non-dual). This key reveals that the first five self-natures are active in various mixtures during everyday life, paving the way for understanding.

We can find solace from self-judgment in that humanity's average is self-interest, family values, and team consciousness. This shared thread binds us all, even as the concept of not fitting in plays a significant role in humanity's cultural evolution from slavery to a global community.

As we progress through the stages, up to the sixth consciousness, certitude, we experience significant reductions in suffering and drama. This journey, a testament to personal growth, is not without its rewards. We often encounter the effortless beauty of synchronicity and come to understand a co-creative strength and responsibility, a realization that can transform our lives.

. . . .

The first stage of consciousness or self-nature, Samudaya, marks the emergence of being driven by collection, possession, and self-interest. This raw, ego-centric identity reflects our survival instinct, shaping our interactions and most of society's everyday interactions. Although rooted in materialism, it is our bravery and transformative power.

Samudaya, translated as the cause of suffering, highlights the pervasive self-interest that fuels fear, societal issues, and personal grief. **Recognizing these limitations is the first step toward transcending them and evolving presence, inclusiveness, and a sense of belonging.**

Despite its primal origins, our first self-nature is not just a product of survival instincts but also the fuel behind self-development and higher consciousness. **By transforming our self-image from one person to oneness with everyone, we also embrace the immense potential** that lies within our primordial self-nature. It's a powerful reminder that even our most primal state of being holds the key to enlightenment, simply with a change of perspective.

. . . .

Bhava, meaning 'being' or 'worldly existence,' represents the second stage of consciousness, characterized by our emotional tendencies and sense of belonging through family and tribe. It emphasizes the importance of relationships and social connections, where our identity is shaped by our affiliations with family, friends, and community.

In this stage, higher values such as loyalty, self-sacrifice, and empathy emerge as we strive to serve the common good and transcend self interest. However, belonging challenges us to broaden our inclusiveness, confronting habits of justification, insecurity, competition, and envy. **Bhava reveals the fragile happiness found in transactional belonging and the cultural beliefs that sustain a sense of identity based on what others think**.

Despite the tendency to resist change and avoid accountability, this stage holds the potential for growth and transformation beyond our dreams.

But the transformative power extends beyond the social structures of family, faith, and community. It is a significant leap in consciousness, as we transcend self-interest and find our place within a collective identity. **The primary challenge lies in overcoming exclusivity and the us-versus-them mentality, which can lead to destructive behavior as seen in our warring world.** By fostering inclusiveness and loving-kindness, we can transform chaos into opportunities, ultimately reaching new heights of devotion, love, and care.

....

The third stage of consciousness, Lakshana signifies the emergence of independent awareness, where we begin to separate ourselves from societal conditioning. This stage, marked by 'not-belonging,' represents a positive turning point in our journey toward self-realization. It is not about isolation but the recognition and understanding of our distinct qualities, allowing us to reject conventional norms and pursue inner truth and freedom.

This stage opens the door to new possibilities, expanding our self-determined willpower and open-mindedness, promising growth and personal liberation.

However, inner revolution is just the beginning. The risk lies in substituting one set of rigid beliefs for another. This self-nature transcends social and cultural norms, fostering moments of awakening and new ways of belonging. **By finding like-minded individuals, we glimpse the potential for societal change**, expanding our understanding and challenging norms to create a more inclusive world.

....

Mahabhuta, within the *Lankavatara Sutra*, signifies the transcendence of material forms and the awakening to formless potential. **This stage moves beyond the belief that material reality is all there is**, introducing the expanse of mind and spirit. Through this awakening, spirituality emerges, laying the foundation for Mindfulness and understanding.

As the fourth kind of self-nature, Mahabhuta translates to the 'great element' or 'primary substance,' encompassing earth, water, fire, air, and space—the elemental forces of all phenomena. This stage represents the building blocks of existence. **Space, as formlessness, relates to consciousness in our emotional awareness, intuition, and subconscious connectivity.** It marks the beginning of awakening, allowing us to perceive deeper significance beyond sensory stimulation.

The challenge is to transcend false-imagination and observe life beyond dualism. **By letting go of desired outcomes and embracing fortune and misfortune with equal gratitude, we cultivate formless awareness.** This stage heralds the emergence of true presence and a vision of reality that surpasses all previous conceptions. It is the dawn of the awakened mind, where loving kindness evolves into acceptance and unconditional love.

. . . .

The fifth self-nature or stage of consciousness is Hetu, Non-dual Rationality. It marks a transformative stage where the unity of all phenomena becomes self-evident. This stage reveals the ultimate cause behind existence as impermanence itself. It provides insights into the nature of reality, helping us understand that all phenomena are without independent existence. **By embracing Non-dual Rationality, we strip away attachment to dualistic questions.**

Understanding these deep connections helps us see beyond superficial appearances, fostering a sense of mental clarity and peace. **But the journey to non-dual awareness is challenging, requiring us to reconcile and discard many comforting beliefs with the stark reality of nature's blameless cause.** This work dissolves judgment and preference, liberating compassion and redefining love as a focus of wisdom and awareness rather than emotional attachment.

Despite its challenges, non-dual awareness offers a connection and understanding at the primordial level. **Hetu encourages us to see beyond physicality and the limits of conventional spirituality,** redirecting our awareness towards empathy, compassion, humility, and gratitude. This shift reestablishes our connection with loving-kindness and guides us to serve others without the intention to change them.

. . . .

Pratyaya the sixth self-nature signifies the certitude of grounded experience in the Absolute, an unwavering conviction born from direct

experience and personal realization. This stage of consciousness integrates all previous experiences, reflecting the synchronicity of life as a seamless flow where one recognizes the non-doer. Here, certitude emerges as a living truth, leading to a state of mental tranquillity and acceptance of all aspects of existence.

Certitude represents the ultimate convergence of objective awareness and loving-kindness, dissolving the boundaries of ego and self-definition. It fosters a serene connection to life, where expectations dissolve, and mindfulness reigns. This stage is marked by the release of personal identity. Through this lens, **Certitude acts as consciousness, highlighting the transient nature of worldly experiences against the backdrop of nature as the blameless cause in a perfectly evolving existence.**

As practitioners journey through the conditions leading to Certitude, such as ethical conduct, meditative absorption, and wisdom, they undergo transformative processes that fundamentally alters their perception of reality. **This journey reflects the shift from conditional existence to the non-dual awareness of the primordial subconscious.** While this state brings profound peace and joy, the ultimate challenge lies in letting go of the attachment to life's pleasures and personal relationships. By embracing deep presence and compassionate acceptance, one achieves a quiet mind and finds freedom in the simple act of letting go.

....

Nishpatti, or Perfect Completion, represents the pinnacle of spiritual attainment, the seventh stage of consciousness or self-nature. It is where individuals transcend all dualities and merge into a state of ecstatic imageless freedom. This journey involves the unification of subconscious and awakened mind. Those who have experienced Nishpatti embody a unified existence beyond roles, relationships, and personal identities, existing solely to serve

26

others without self-interest. **They are likened to perfect mirrors reflecting the essence of unconditional love and compassion.**

In this state of Perfect Completion, individuals transcend the conventional notions of belonging, embracing a reality where personality gives way to a pure reflection

While traditional descriptions of Nishpatti emphasize liberation from the cycle of birth and death, modern interpretations suggest a broader application. **This inclusive vision of enlightenment encourages us to continue striving for greater awareness and compassion,** fostering a collective journey towards peace and harmony amidst the complexities of contemporary life.

Being Human, OWM

Thou art a human-being, in this life's play, where sense-consciousness gathers, day by day. Human-collecting covets thoughts and things, while human-doing acts, thinks, and brings.

Yet thou art human-being, meant to be, the quiet weaver, of all you see. Mindful suchness, where nothing clings, orchestrate consciousness, on artful wings.

Freedom's vision, relax their hold, empty, free of stories untold. No collecting, doing, judging art molded, serenity sees life as unfolded.

Oneness weaves through every harp string, in suchness and resonance all things they do sing. Thou art that, the quiet embrace, human-being, in timeless effortless grace.

Stars whisper secrets in the night, embracing darkness, revealing light.

Gaia's pulse, a cosmic rhyme, in every breath, transcending time. Here lies the end.

The stages of consciousness or self-natures guide us to a deeper sense of unity, revealing the interconnectedness of all existence. By perceiving the essence of all things, we realize that what hurts one, hurts all, and what heals one, heals all, fostering a powerful sense of empathy.

Understanding the evolution of consciousness through identity, presence, and inclusiveness, we can transform these concepts into the awakened mind, known as Bodhicitta.

This universal journey of awareness, alive in everyone, builds layers of subtle understanding, guiding us from a focus on self to a broader comprehension of humanity, compassion, spirituality, and ultimately, Buddhahood.

Joanne Mitchell (my wife and principal editor)

We are all connected to all that is, as facets of the one.

All made of the same fabric, magnificently, uniquely individualized like every snowflake… If they melt, they lose individuation and return to source, water or vapor…

Demonstrating just a temporary illusion of separateness.

Lanka: Sagathakam, sloka

675. As we search out failures and defects, the principle is not found. Even the mind fails to serve, as its dualistic functions are mere appearance. **Non-duality is suchness, itself.**

Mirror, OWM

A finger may not touch itself. An eye may not see itself. The mind grapples its own airy form, beyond the brain, where thoughts transform.

Differences sensed, sameness missed, our tool of thought, meaning kissed. Yet thinking can't perceive its own, unawareness blooms where seeds are sown.

Depth overlooked in life's vast sea, chasing illusions, missing the glee. Images held, like dust in flight, sunset restrained, in futile fight.

Love and acceptance, the fearless might, dissolve the doubt in certain light. Inside-out, as the journey goes, within, the source of love, mind flows. Thou art the Buddha, clear of mind, no preferences, no judgments there to blind.

The seven stages of consciousness has eluded me until now. The first few stages seem clear, but it's the higher levels, like non-dual awareness, certitude, and Buddhahood, that I find intriguing and challenging to understand.

The problem is that everyone I know and love could be categorized primarily into the first three stages of consciousness. These stages, which are often associated with senses, preferences, and thinking about the physical world, are where most people reside. **But that's the interesting part because my awakening is repeatedly described by the *Lanka*, as seeing the awakening in others.** So, maybe they have a lot more going on than I recognize, until I inquire more deeply. Until they let me in.

Have you ever taken a moment to truly appreciate the wisdom that exists within those you love? It's a powerful and often overlooked source of insight that can enrich our lives in ways we might not expect.

Let's delve into the the seven stages of consciousness. What aspects can we relate to? What seems distant? **Understanding these stages sparks a curiosity in me to look beyond my habitual reactions and encourages me to see the awakening potential, especially others.**

The next chapter will present a vastly simplified version of Ravana's sudden awakening and many unusual concepts. But don't struggle and dig out a dictionary; just let the terms wash over you, and slowly, they will be clarified in context.

Being esoteric raises questions of encoding and hidden knowledge. Does it make sense that something is also esoteric because it is beyond our experience and so, beyond our understanding? Nothing is intentionally hidden here.

CHAPTER FIVE
Sudden Awakening

In the journey of a seeker, moments of sudden awakening can strike with the force of a lightning bolt, illuminating the deepest recesses of our consciousness. This chapter draws us into the enlightened wisdom of the ancient *Lanka*. It delves into the realization that words and rational thought fall short of capturing the highest reality. Instead, it is through the three pillars of Noble Wisdom: 'imagelessness ', 'transmission ', and 'self-realization ', that we experience bliss and unity.

'Imagelessness' refers to the transcendence of form, 'transmission' to the direct communication of spiritual truths, and 'self-realization' to the awakening of our true nature.

As we traverse the path laid out by Ravana's awakening, we are invited to reflect on our own experiences and the transformative power of surrendering to our higher self.

Lanka: Chapter 2, Section XXXIII

Words are not the highest reality, nor can truth or ultimate reality be contained in words. To experience absolute truth or the highest reality is an exalted state of bliss, not accessible by mere description. It is found in the realm of imagelessness, transmission, and self-realization, the three steps of Noble Wisdom. Ascended and realized at the deepest level, oneness gives birth to the highest bliss, diving into the womb of enlightenment, the subconscious, Alaya.

Lanka: Sagathakam, slokas

266. *The cultivated man or woman, despite their efforts, often find themselves standing on the truth of their own knowing, unable to fully comprehend the essence of things or the vast plane of unknowns.*

They profess brilliant ideas, such as the laws of physics or the theory of evolution, based on what can be known and sensed. Yet, the ultimate truth, like a mirage, always seems to shimmer just beyond their reach, limited by the filter of cognition and the absence of intuitive, unchanging knowledge. Truth is abandoned, not due to lack of effort, but for lack of penetration.

267. *The twin adversaries of self-deception and ignorance, which afflict us all, are the only barriers to be surmounted. The illusion of a 'separate self', the ego perception, or who I perceive myself to be, is the veil that needs to be lifted. **Once the unity of all things is discerned, no malevolent thought lingers for the world.***

268. *Scholars often depict an eternal creator in their teachings. But have you ever pondered, the highest truth is beyond the confines of language? It is inherently grasped within the serene mind of 'suchness ', a notion that surpasses our linguistic boundaries.*

269. *Drawing on the subconscious Alaya, the subjective mind wills and discriminates depending on its accumulation and awareness. **The higher mind is another name for awareness; through it, consciousness evolves.***

270. *An idea only establishes a proposition, but 'suchness', a term referring to the true nature of reality, is an essence. When grasped, it gives the Yogin, a mind-only awareness.*

In the following transliterations, we hear the main part of Ravana's Sudden Awakening.

Lanka: **Chapter 1, Alaya Consciousness**

Buddha's teachings echo, "The awakened ones, who have gone before, are worthy of our praise. ***They taught us that the subconscious is not a distant realm, but our very own access to the vast ocean of all knowledge (Alaya).*** *This door opens to imagelessness, transmission, and self-realization, the heart of Noble Wisdom. It surpasses rational understanding and even the enlightened mind, yet it is only veiled within our identity as personality or self. I am here to empower you with this knowledge."*

Lanka: **Chapter 1, The mirror of self**

19. Buddha, Master of the three worlds, said, "Ravana, King of Nature Spirits, this realm of intelligence and abundance has been visited by great visionaries in the past."

*20. "**Having compassion for you, they exposed your understanding to the truth of their own self-realization**, as will the enlightened also proclaim the great way to future generations."*

21. "Indeed, great masters of discipline, have attained the shelter of faith-mind, tranquillity, by observing the world from non-judgment. You, the master of worldliness, can also find it within yourself through the love and wisdom of avatars and the enlightened."

In this part of Ravana's story, the Lord of Lanka is pushed to breaking point, as the **Buddha ignores him until he surrenders to the higher self (Mahamati).** Buddha is finally convinced of Ravana's sincerity and begins to engage.

Lanka: **Chapter 1, Sudden Awakening**

The Higher Self says:

30. "Liberated from the enlightenment of mind, doctrine, and discrimination, the mistakes of rationality are no more. The truth of Buddha-nature is flawless, leading to subconscious transformation and unified consciousness."

*31. On hearing this, **the Buddha manifested innumerable mountain Kingdoms**, bejeweled with intelligence, abundance, and wealth, with the most valuable objects and attainments of a material world.*

32. Buddha, Ravana and all the nature spirits appeared standing above every kingdom as Lords of the earth.

*33. So, the Buddha, Ravana, and their companions were recognized as the highest authority in each kingdom, attended and served by the ruler of every land. **Ravana is stunned and amazed when the scene changes to fulfil his secret, most grandiose desire: to be lord of the world.***

34. Here stood the lord of man's lower nature, Ravana, and all his kingdom of nature spirits worshipping him. The Buddha conjured even the city of Lanka countless times for all to see.

35. Every aspect was perfect. Even the palace and royal pleasure gardens appeared on every mountain peak. Then also Mahamati, the Higher Self, was seen appealing to the Buddha, just as Ravana had desired.

36. To complete every wish Ravana expressed, the Buddha disclosed the great way for all beings to understand. He revealed the truth in each kingdom according to each individual's ability, intelligence, and circumstance.

*37. **As the teaching concluded, everything and everyone vanished, leaving Ravana in solitude with his thoughts.***

The impact of being utterly alone is like a bomb detonating, and a storm of questions consumes Ravana!

38. *Ravana is thrown into a whirlwind of thoughts, "What was that? What does it signify?* **Am I hallucinating or losing my mind?** *What about everyone else?* **Did they perceive my grandiose desires?** *The city, the people and all the kingdoms were tangible. Even the Buddha was teaching, as I requested."*

39. *"Where are the kings and princes of humanity, or the host of enlightened beings and God men?* **Was this a dream, a delusion, or a spell cast by spirits?"**

40. *"**Maybe I have some kind of physical impairment**, or it was some kind of mirage? If it's not my own wishful thinking, maybe it was the ghostly image of something that once existed."*

How do we gain wisdom in life? Growing up, the notions of childhood were largely destroyed, and even as an adult, the collapse of romantic idealism was the most outstanding teacher to instruct me on love. Do you see your sudden awakening in the steps along the path of your life?

As Chapter Five draws to a close, we are left to ponder the essence of Ravana's awakening. His journey from self-deception mirrors our own struggles and triumphs. **The fleeting grandeur experienced by Ravana serves as a poignant reminder of the impermanence of worldly desires and the ultimate truth that lies beyond them.** In our own lives, **the moments of sudden awakening are often marked by a shattering of illusions and a deepening of understanding.** Through these experiences, we are invited to transcend the limits of rational thought and embrace the boundless wisdom of the subconscious. But the story doesn't end here, it just begins and now Ravana is ready to hear what few have understood.

CHAPTER SIX
Lucid Awareness

In the depths of spiritual exploration, a moment arrives when clarity cuts through the fog of confusion and illusion. This chapter serves as a guide, leading us through Ravana's transformative journey from rational emptiness to a discerning state of lucidity.

Through the teachings of the Buddha, Ravana learns to transcend the limitations of belief and disbelief, embracing a reality that lies beyond the constructs of the rational mind.

Ravana is left in a state of rational emptiness after reflecting on the shock, horror, and awe he experienced, leading to clarity and lucidity.

Lanka: Chapter 1, Suchness

*41. Ravana experiences non-cognitive awareness, "It's all my mind's creation. I have seen and experienced the drama of life's highest lesson playing out in everyone's life. Not understanding this, **others fail to recognize the pattern of oneness behind form.**"*

42. "In this realization, there is neither one who sees nor that which is seen. It is not taught, for it cannot be spoken. Even the Buddha, his actions and his truth—are nothing, but what the mind creates."

*43. "Others having shared this experience, do not see the blessed one through belief. The Buddha cannot be seen. **The fully enlightened may only be witnessed prior to perception, thinking and doing.** Only then do the*

Buddhas show themselves, when the mind is not agitated nor conflicted in doing or being."

Buddha addressing Ravana for the first time:

*"**Well done, Ravana! …seeing the awakened and everything without the limits of belief or disbelief, you validate the truth of intuitive awareness**. As you have experienced, reality is going beyond the exclusions created by will, memory, thought, senses and awareness. Going within, **do not tie yourself to doctrine or accept the world's view at face value.** Avoid the seduction of achievements, which can be a limiting goal."*

"Avoid demeaning others and all distinctions of separateness such as entitlement or self-interest. Do not seek fame, glory, or clairvoyance. Only arising naturally can they contain authenticity."

*"**Mind-only, discovered by the Yogins, renders the habit of belief as oblivious baggage, while eliminating the fearful views of life**. This triumph, called Sudden Awakening, uncovers the higher-self, beyond the limits of false identification. In this way, thoughts of self-interest become repulsive and shameful. In this mindfulness, nothing in life needs to change, but everything is transformed as the awareness shifts to one's core being. This is the great way, through which all must pass, in realizing their true self."*

The Awakened Self (Buddha) continues in a fatherly tone:

*"Understanding reality, as the creation of one's mind, conviction and certainty follow experience of the absolute. Through practice, unselfish intentions and proper identification of self, manifestations are seen to be thought constructions only. **This attainment is an exquisite magical thinking, leading to the most incredible and magnificent life.**"*

38

Buddha counsels, "The veil is lifted as obsession with self fades. Noisy internal dialog subsides, absent the defence of beliefs. The struggle ends, as does shame, blame, and all external causes.

But beware of paths thinly masking self-interest as bait. The consequence of the slightest separateness or self-importance leads to endless cycles of false hope and misery."

"Congratulations, Lord Ravana, you have correctly embraced awakening."

Lanka: Sagathakam, sloka

882. **When the sudden awakening blooms from the inmost revulsion of discrimination, death and destruction lose all significance**, *laughing, he talks of truth and enlightenment, knowing its imaginary illusion with a brilliance like no other gem.*

The First Cause, OWM

Impermanence whispers, the eternal dance, time's fleeting touch, each day's advance. Stars guide, time turns the wheel, water's flow, in ceaseless reel.

Life and death, intertwined symphony, endless cycle, no final decree. With each breath, creation's spark, life devours, and death leaves its mark.

Embrace death's embrace, impermanence its broader face.

Forms shift, energy echoes loud, not lost, but reborn in every cloud.

Today, embrace life's closing sigh, release regrets, let resolutions fly.

Right wrongs, let love's song resound, In sleep's embrace, dreams profound. No divisions, in that nightly place, where names fade, and souls embrace.

Everywhere, you remain unchanged, in dreams' realm, no need restrained.

Lanka: **Chapter 2, Section XIV**

The refinement of people, cultural behaviors, and attitudes is a gradual and progressive process, much like gardening, with its various seasons for planting, growing, and harvesting. Similarly, **the purification of beings by the Buddha is a gradual process and not an instantaneous one.**

Breaking the shell of compulsive habitual thinking is not an instantaneous process until the moment of sudden awakening. This moment is like the sun in mid-sky on a cloudless day, where every form, from every direction, is revealed without a shadow.

This experience of imagelessness arises by eliminating the habit of reacting from judgment and opinion. *It reveals a domain of unthinkable innate knowledge, as if the subconscious recreates the world anew.*

The Buddha discards addictive habits from which false imaginations arise. Here, intuition and awareness of synchronicity reveal the realm of unimaginable surprise and mystery.

As the subconscious becomes unencumbered, it reveals a world of effortless being and infinite co-creativity. *The not-separate relationship of oneness shows the mutuality of eternal, impermanent, and interdependent existence, where conscious awareness of synchronicity is the ground of being. Imagelessness arises first on the road of sudden awakening, which may be instantaneous but impermanent.* **It is the practice of Mind-only that penetrates the subconscious fabric.** *It appears to arise as a gradual enlightenment, slowly reshaping the subconscious.*

Letting Go, **OWM**

Love blooms bright, with passion's fire, yet fades with time, as hearts retire.

All that's held is fleeting, seen in its glow, suffering emerges where stories flow. Choose not to weave, no suffering near, release the grip, let it disappear.

"No appointment, no disappointment," they say, in resonant chords, all find their way. In innocence lies, beloved and free, **see only love, and that it will be.**

Love wholly, let go without chain, embrace the freedom, to let it reign. Plans unfold, impeded by will, acceptance blooms, serene and still.

Born of blood, bone, more and less this shell, life's lifeforce pulses, beyond its spell. From sensing thought, preference springs, concepts gathered as experience sings.

Human life questions, what more to find, in just being, beyond the mind? Freedom from compulsion's control, to see beyond habit, where souls unroll.

No judgment, no offense, no 'me' to bind, in effortless living, true peace to find. Being human, embracing suchness true, beyond senses and concepts, a deeper view.

In the present's flow, awareness grows, beyond discrimination, where stillness shows. No right, no wrong, no this, nor that, just the quiet voice, where truth is at.

To be here, fully present, in unity's hush, where oneness resides, in stillness plush.

We find Ravana standing on the precipice of a new understanding. His journey through shock, horror, and awe has led him to a place of unparalleled clarity and lucidity. The teachings of the Buddha illuminate the path to true awareness, where the mind transcends its habitual confines and embraces the oneness of all existence. This state of lucid awareness is not merely an intellectual achievement but a deep experiential reality, accessible to those who dare to look beyond the surface of perception.

As we close this chapter, investigate your own inspiration and moments of sudden awakening. Break free from preconceived notions and limited understanding, to realize the boundless, interconnected reality that awaits us all.

CHAPTER SEVEN
Duality

In the path of conscious existence, we often find ourselves ensnared by the concept of duality—dividing the world into opposites. This chapter explores the profound teachings of the Buddha as he guides Ravana through the labyrinth of dualistic thought. Through this journey, we come to understand that the mind's reliance on opposites to structure knowledge is a source of both clarity and confusion.

As we delve into this chapter, **we are challenged to transcend the limitations of dualistic thinking and embrace a holistic awareness that reveals the interconnectedness of all things.**

Lanka: **D.T. Suzuki, Epistemology**

The mind structures knowledge in opposites to define its related pair and understand the relative world, such as heaven and hell, good and evil, life and death, etc. ***This dualistic structure provides us with judgment based on concepts we create.*** *However, the mind loses track of what comes from what, so that truth and wrong judgment can become indistinguishable as complexities compile into chaos.* ***Clinging to this as reality from birth, even the subconscious cannot extricate itself from the bog of judgment, opinion, likes, and dislikes.***

In the next section we return to the story of Ravana's Sudden Awakening. These are the questions he wished to ask upon completion of his awakening.

Lanka: **Chapter 1, Duality questioned**

In a moment of serious contemplation, Ravana asked the Buddha, *"Duality, rarely understood, has never been explained by a Buddha of the subconscious primordial depths.* Such Buddhas, absorbed in bliss and emptiness, shun trivial matters since they neither judge dualism nor instruct on it. "...

"We have been told, to embrace the non-dual, one must abandon truth and untruth. Why must definitions be relinquished? How is it even possible? Truth and untruth may be easy because they are vague abstractions. But how can we dismiss the function of our awareness to perceive the world?"

"We understand the delusion of Duality as the divisive discrimination of circumstance and the isolating fear of others. We objectify life and misidentify ideas of what is real or not. Duality belongs to the realm of abstraction, and intellectual creation. How can one even fathom abandonment of Duality as truth or untruth?"

Lanka: Chapter 1, Delusion

Buddha, in response to Ravana's query on duality, presented a paradox: "Fire, in its indiscriminate nature, consumes everything from shacks to castles, parks to forests. Yet, the colors of its flame and the intensity of its ferocity vary, contingent upon the structure and energy of its fuel. This is an undeniable truth. But why do we fail to grasp that our equality as human beings does not equate to a uniform understanding? It is our attachment to trivial, ignorant desires that births the dichotomy of truth and untruth."

"As one Fire expands and becomes many, a single seed produces one plant with all its component parts. The stem, leaves, flowers, fruit, and branches share a common life and yet are each individualized; no two are the same."

"External life grows in the same way as internal life. From who we think we are, we develop obsessions with the body, emotions, perceptions, thought, and consciousness. Even intuition from this bias of self is false-imagination."

"As we can cling equally to healthy and unhealthy things or experiences, these compulsions grow from desire, form, and formlessness. What we perceive to be happiness, appearance, expression, and conduct, are all arising continuously around us but beyond our control."

"So, it makes sense that our identification with consciousness is experienced differently, dependent on what we can verify in a physical world. *We see things as good and bad, better and worse, pure and unclean. Not only are there infinite variations on the conditions and forms of life in general, but also the inner experience and realizations of everyone vary extremely, even as he or she treads the well-established path of good practice."*

"Do you think we create our own great chasms, between truth and untruth, in our compulsive world of self, characteristically enslaved by discrimination? You bet we do!"

Brilliance Beyond, OWM

Rational man, bound in thought's confine, imagines reality, yet misses the sign. **The magic of oneness, a mystic delight, to him seems nonsense, lost from sight.**

Enslaved by habits of rational lore, all things appear as they've always before. Reality's illusion, a separate domain, projecting thoughts in a self-made frame.

Infatuated with the physical, he claims, all that exists in tangible names. Identifying constructs of thought as the self, he shelves the magic on a dusty shelf.

Lanka: **Chapter 1, Validity**

The Awakened Self, Buddha defines detachment,

"Lord Ravana, the separation and distinctions of truth and untruth are only products of prejudice and opinion. What do we commonly believe as truth? They are judgments based on memory and opinion, handed down and defended by those most invested in their perpetuation.

This pre-judging leads us to believe that truth, understood to have value and meaning, comes from an ultimate source or cause, but you should always question these notions. *Such truths can generally not be upheld as unavoidable reality because they are only characteristics and features by which a thing is recognized.*

Clinging to this perspective comes from regarding your outcomes of thought as reality. *These thoughts are self-limiting containers, products of our belief and imagination, conceived in need, desire, and limitation without our full awareness. They don't exist separate from our prejudice because their substance is not independent of our projection.*

To understand things from this perspective is known as detachment or abandonment."

Lanka: **Chapter 1, Abandoning Duality**

The Awakened Self, Buddha continues:

46

"Okay, Ravana. What are untruths? Argue as you may, untruths are only beliefs, dislikes, and disagreements that cannot be proven and come from no absolute cause. As you said, truth and untruth are abstractions and projections. Their reality or fantasy is unreliable, lacking physicality and verification.

This idea is known as abandoning truth and untruth.

So, why are truths beyond verification and comprehension? Very often, they are just imaginings, like unicorns, the Easter Bunny, Eeyore the donkey, or a horned camel. Sometimes, we also imagine truths from wishful thinking, like the heartfelt longing of a barren woman to have her own child.

All truth's essential nature is unreachable, so we say, "We must take them on faith." However, such faith is often the veil of control by others, and truth should not be thought of as certain because truths and untruths are only the façade of something and not the real thing itself.

Truth or untruth should be embraced only if it makes sense universally. It should never be imposed as a substantive reality or as boundaries to limit understanding. Some 'truths,' given an artistic value in our thinking, maybe disconnected entirely from substantive reality. Here, detachment or abandonment makes sense.

As we venture deeper into the realm of these intangible thoughts, the certainty of their existence begins to fade. In this light, letting go of things that stem from discrimination and prejudice becomes a natural progression of our awareness. This perspective is the essence of 'abandoning truth and untruth'. Lord Ravana, I believe your question has now been thoroughly addressed.

The Buddha imparts teachings that transcend ordinary understanding, emphasizing the direct perception of ultimate reality. Through this encounter, Ravana is guided to look beyond dualistic thinking and intellectual concepts, directly experiencing the true nature of his own consciousness. This sudden and transformative realization reveals our interconnectedness and the illusory nature of separations.

The teachings of the Buddha illuminate a path to liberation, demonstrating that true enlightenment lies in recognizing life's oneness and the mind's essential nature. This journey inspires us, not only to seek our own direct realization, but also to realize the potential for liberation that lies within us. It reminds us that the ultimate truth is beyond words and concepts, empowering us to embark on our own sudden awakening.

As we conclude the chapter on Duality, we are left with a transformative insight into the nature of reality. Ravana's journey serves as an example for our own spiritual quests. **The teachings of the Buddha reveal that the distinctions we cling to are constructs of the mind, products of prejudice and opinion.**

By embracing detachment and abandoning the white-knuckled grip on belief as truth or untruth, we liberate ourselves from the constraints of judgment and open ourselves to a unified consciousness. This chapter challenges all of us to let go of our habitual judgments and to see beyond the distinctions and separations that cloud our perception. **In doing so, we move closer to the ultimate truth, a truth that transcends words and concepts, residing within the depths of our own being, fostering our sense of liberation.**

CHAPTER EIGHT
Beyond Duality

In this chapter we journey deeper into the teachings of enlightened awareness. It opens with the Awakened Self addressing Ravana, the ever-curious seeker, urging him to transcend the confines of dualistic thinking.

But, **the Buddha's teachings focus on the dissolution of conceptual barriers that bind human perception to limited frameworks of time, space, and form.** Through complex dialogues and poetic expressions, we are guided to explore the essence of "suchness", a state of pure, non-prejudiced awareness that lies beyond conventional discriminations.

This chapter also delves into the nature of true enlightenment, illustrating how the enlightened beings, free from judgment and self-identity, embody a reality where wisdom, love, and oneness flow effortlessly. **As we navigate through these insights, we are invited to witness the magic of life unencumbered by attachments** and to recognize the infinite potential of the human spirit when aligned with transcendental wisdom.

Lanka: **Chapter 1, Beyond words**

The Awakened Self turns to Ravana to see if he understands the teachings. Ravana appears a bit uncertain, but his eyes are alert, indicating his readiness to learn.

The Buddha continues:

*"Now Ravana, let's delve deeper into our exploration. **Remember, we were just playing with words in the first place.** You mentioned these questions had*

been asked of other enlightened beings in the past, who answered them. But when we speak of the past, isn't it just another concept, dividing and defining it from future or present, mere discriminations of time?

*Living in a serene reality, **enlightened beings** transcend judgment. They **go beyond discrimination and pointless rationalizations, which include time, space, and form.** Yet, they do represent reality as separate appearances but only for the benefit of sentient beings, as a context for suchness and humanities' peaceful wellbeing.*

'Suchness ' refers to the true nature of things beyond conceptualization and discrimination.** It is a state of non-prejudiced, non-conceptual awareness, and it is from this awareness that the Buddhas teach effortless belonging beyond cause, form, and the discriminations of time and space because that is their essential state of being. **But, suchness itself is also just discrimination. Because, lacking prejudice, it is also non-conceptual awareness, and as such, it is discernment at the highest level.

The enlightened, with their seemingly magical abilities, can captivate us with their knowledge of our lives or their ability to be in multiple places at once. Yet, to them, it's not magic, it is hearing, seeing, or moving by a subtle resonance, without the limits of discrimination, evolved from loving kindness and an untainted intuitive insight. They live in and have as their essence transcendental wisdom.

***The enlightened Buddhas, are free from the shackles of judgment and discrimination. So, they cannot be judged or understood according to identity, personality, or ego.** The reason they do not judge thought itself is because discrimination only arises from the identification with a separate self, a soul, or a personality. This freedom from judgment is a source of inspiration and liberation.*

How do enlightened beings rise above the realms of judgment and opinion? They reside in their limitless selves, beyond the confines of the subjective, attached mind. **Liberated from self-will and ownership, their thoughts are unrestricted, drawing freely from Alaya, the subconscious living field of all life, the wellspring of all knowledge, and the Dharma itself.**

Balance, OWM

The vast subconscious, steadfast guide, stands beside you, a resource wide. Senses as guardians, loyal and true, ensuring safety, with peace imbue.

In quietude's embrace, desires unfold, acceptance blooms, as you behold. Belonging not a strife-filled quest, but effortless grace, where hearts find rest.

Release the struggle, let go of dues, give freely, all you touch accrues. Life's stream flows, waves of magic unfold, witness them whole, not parts untold. Thou art the witness, serene and clear, in life's changing waves, always near. Love's essence, misunderstood by some, it springs from you, a boundless hum.

Love knows no bounds, it freely flows, embracing all, each life it shows. Age and circumstance, no divide, in love's warm embrace, all may reside.

Lanka: Chapter 1, Humanities' potential

The 'awakened self,' through heightened consciousness and self-realization, continues,

"Though the subjective, attached mind is meant for the material world, infatuation overpowers us with form, appearance, and value. *This desire separates us from our true potential.*

Lord Ravana, the lives of most human beings are mere images of what they could be, lacking sensibility and a real awareness of life. Everything in their world of appearance is devoid of significance because people lack meaning and purpose. They cannot be taught because no one is interested until they have cause through awakening, usually by significant loss.

However, all this can change in the flash of a moment, magically transformed, though not understood as possible by intellectuals and those limited to judgment and discrimination.

Seeing beyond appearance and judgment is to see truthfully. Seeing otherwise is to depend on likes, dislikes, prejudice, and the fear of losing a make-believe image. Grasping this, repulsed by that, jumping to conclusions, and living in unspoken fear, we become enmeshed in mental agitations, only waves, and foam on a vast ocean.

The images we create are only shadows of our true selves, like confusing oneself with one's reflection in a mirror or believing the echo in a valley is your authentic voice. *Clinging to shadows, we defend our beliefs, which include truth and untruth.* Not recognizing our projections, we continue in a life dictated by ignorant desire and never know peace.

Peace is oneness. Knowing our greater self, as a focal point in the living field of all life's intelligence, is knowing no one as separate from anyone else. Oneness gives birth to the highest bliss, diving into the womb of enlightenment, the subconscious, Alaya. *This transcendence is the magic of meditation.* Here lies the realm of imagelessness, transmission, and self-realization."

Concluding with a powerful reminder of every human being's boundless potential, we understand that true enlightenment transcends the superficial divisions of time, space, and ego. **The Buddha's teachings emphasize that peace and oneness arise from recognizing our most profound connection to the living field of all life, Alaya.** These transcriptions from the *Lanka* beautifully articulate that the journey toward enlightenment is not about accumulating knowledge or skills but shedding the layers of discrimination and judgment that obscure our true nature. By embracing non-conceptual awareness or suchness, self-realization arises naturally as we align ourselves with limitless wisdom and compassion.

As we close this chapter, we are left with an inspiring vision of human potential, one where love, peace, and unity prevail and where each individual can tap into the depths of their being to experience their highest potential of oneness in the magic of life.

CHAPTER NINE
The Structures of Mind

Here we delve into the convoluted structures of the mind, exploring the elements that shape our consciousness and perception. This chapter invites readers to journey beyond the surface of everyday awareness into the deeper realms of human psychology as understood through the lens of ancient Buddhist teachings.

Here, we uncover how the interplay of the subconscious, sensory perception, and conceptual thought constructs our experience of reality. **By examining the processes described in the *Lanka*, we aim to reveal** the subtle mechanisms of mind that govern our lives, offering insights into **how we can transcend habitual patterns and awaken to a life beyond our dreams.** Through this exploration, we aspire to illuminate the path toward self-awareness and a deeper understanding of our true nature.

Lanka: Sagathakam, slokas

> *157. During conception, the parent's subconscious life force infuses the fertilized egg's first seed of consciousness, growing in red and white tissues to create a sentient being from the living field.*

Each cell duplication creates repeated entanglement of energy in every other cell. **Physical sensation is mutual for the daughter cells, and experience is shared synchronistically (instantaneously, regardless of distance).** This entangled mutuality is the basis of the life force discovered in Quantum Mechanics about a hundred years ago.

Lanka: Sagathakam, slokas

158. The stages of growth, seemingly straightforward, are in fact the enigmatic process of life's creation. **With subconscious tendencies, disposition, and inheritance, the intangible transmission of life force manifests as DNA, cells, organs, systems, and structure.**

159. The five elements, earth, water, fire, air, and ether, interact with the five senses, sight, hearing, touch, taste, and smell-and the five aspects of sentience, form, sensation, perception, cognition, and sense consciousness. They develop the nine vital organs, bringing forth a sentient being.

160. This form of flesh and blood is a consequence of natural law. **Waking as from a dream, the eye distinguishes light, and discrimination grows from form to sensation, to preference, to concept, and finally sentient awareness.**

161. The journey of awareness is a transformative one, evolving into knowledge and speech through the act of parroting what is heard. These are the patterns of discrimination, the echoes of our carers, that shape our understanding of the world.

Entangled mutuality or **life force is a function of countless energetic entanglements occurring during cell division**, so that changes in each cell are felt mutually and simultaneously within every other cell, according to structure and function. **Our cells need few instructions and little communications because they feel what others feel energetically, the mutual experience as one life form.** This life force creates structures such as organs, nerves, fluids and hormones according to its energetic field.

Ancient Buddhism's five elements are earth, air, water, fire, and space, the spiritual sky. Sentient beings' five aspects are the accumulation of sense consciousness, indicated in sloka 160 and expanded below.

The Endless Loop

An egg, a symbol of life's potential, infused with a force essential.
Heartbeat's rhythm, first sensation, in this pulse, existence's foundation.
Life flows, sustenance unfolds, some pleasant (yum), others cold (yuk), bold. Neutral balance, swaying none, preference in difference, duality begun.

Repetition molds, habits form, concepts take shape, norm to norm. Sense of self begins to dawn, names assigned, distinctions drawn.

Sense-consciousness seeks its thrill, pleasure, excitement, protection fulfill. Identification insecure, thought constructions cling, craving, suffering, these attachments bring.

Addicted to self, ideas enslaved, by narratives self-built, vision depraved. Potential stunted, desperation rife, holding on seems all of life.

Bound by names, forms, ideas grand, lifetimes entangled, like grains of sand. Yet in the child, new minds rise, patterns discerned, truth in disguise.

Clinging's fault seen, objectively clear, intuitive knowledge, unchanging and near. Beyond names, stories that bind, in stillness, suchness, truth we find.

Cascading thoughts set adrift, thou art that, the ultimate gift.

Lanka: Chapter 2, section LII

*Sentient beings, including humans, are characterized through five aspects of thought construction (Skandhas). These include form, sensation, preference, concept and sense-consciousness. 'Form' in this context refers to the physical body, which is the only aspect with physical substantiality. The **rest,*** *including that which is unique to the individual, exists only in the formlessness of mind.*

*Beginning with sensation, each sentient being develops the preferences of likes, dislikes, and apathy. With repetition, these preferences become patterns of thought and then concepts. **All these thought constructions become a collection of sense-consciousness to integrate our five senses.***

With their discerning eyes, the wise perceive these aspects, including form, as the ephemeral creations of the mind.. As such, they are known to hinder the understanding of one's true self, with the preoccupation of individuality and the fascination with form.

But these thought constructions are not to be blamed for our suffering.** They are only reflections of the variety of experience, which define our sentient lives. Mastering them is recognition and awareness to enforce an identification with **solitude, a state of introspection and self-awareness, which reserves the right to observe and consciously choose what the variety of experience will be and what it means.

Understanding the construction of sense-consciousness without ego or individual desires purifies the path to enter the stage of Far-going. Herein lies the path to meditative consciousness, the will to discern illusion, and understanding the basis of animal sense construction. However, the human potential beyond sense-consciousness may naturally blossom into intuitive perception, a fascinating realm that may manifest as paranormal powers, serving as a unique means to benefit others.

Lanka: **Chapter 6, section LXXXVII**

The five aspects of sentient beings (Skandhas) are the collection mechanisms through the habits of memory, thought, and identification

with mind as self. They are only imagined to be good or bad through our preferences, which shape our perception. However, true happiness, peace, joy, and awakening can be found in accepting and loving the existing world just as it is, without struggle. This method of awakening only requires acceptance, suchness, and loving-kindness, enlightening us to the power of our preferences in shaping our reality.

Beyond Collection, OWM

Form, a vessel for sensation's flow, gathers thought, lets ideas grow.

Patterns woven, concepts spun, preferences form, yet truth is none.

Sense-consciousness from form is born, But thou art not of form's adorn.

Beyond this realm of fleeting sense, thy essence lies, immense, immense.

The journey starts, collection's creed, thoughts take shape, in patterns breed.

Habit and pattern seen as whole, repetition's trap consumes the soul.

Thou art not form, nor sense, nor thought, nor prejudice with which we're taught. **Collection's living, both wood and water, yet life is more, more rich and broader.**

Thou art life, profound and vast, a complex being, first and last.

Transcending what's gathered here, thou art all life beyond the mere.

Lanka: Chapter 2, section IV

Consciousness reveals itself through its dynamic relationship with the physical world. Its essence is discerned through its actions and influences. ***These actions manifest in three distinct modes, two for our daily interactions, and one for our conscious evolution.*** *The first mode involves the indiscriminate collection of concepts, experiences, emotions, and material things. The second mode is characterized by the creation of cause* and effect, the execution of tasks, and the initiation of action. However, **the third mode of consciousness truly captivates us, as it piques our curiosity by contemplating the inherent nature of suchness, untouched by the acts of collecting or doing.**

When our waking consciousness diverges from our individuated subconscious, their discord is not pacified by the collective subconscious, Alaya. However, when these two aspects of our consciousness align, they attain a peaceful slumber. Yet, it's important to note that the collective subconscious, always active, continues to operate, even during our rest and sleep, sparking our thoughts and contemplation.

Only the waking sense consciousness experiences change or disturbance with subconscious disharmony. Also, when sense consciousness ceases to function, the individuated subconscious ceases, though not the collective subconscious.

However, ceasing the individuated subconscious seems no different from the 'nihilistic disbelief', a term used to describe the rejection of all religious and moral principles, in reincarnation or the metaphysics of continuation.

The nihilist, analytical man or woman says, "When discernment of the objective world ceases, consciousness has stopped entirely. So, the collective subconscious is also destroyed."

However, this perspective is limited to what may be seen and measured while assuming a 'first cause,' a term used to describe the initial event or cause that sets off a chain of causation, such as the soul, God, time, or the atom.

They need help understanding the living intelligence of life itself, 'entangled mutuality,' which refers to the fabric of interconnectedness and interdependence of all things co-arising. Beyond words and without cause, *continuation may only be expressed in understanding that eye consciousness occurs from the simple interaction of form and light. So, too, with hearing, taste, touch, and smell.* ***The misperception is to assume a form-dependence or first cause of sense-consciousness and a non-energetic mechanism for the subconscious.***

Without first cause or form dependence, no discrimination exists, and a new awareness, full of potential and possibilities, is available, inspiring us to explore the depths of consciousness.

This section leans over the wall of rational discernment, inviting us to explore the concepts of entangled mutuality, synchronicity, and the living intelligence of life itself. These terms, which transcend the limitations of our language, touch upon the very essence of what we often refer to as the divine. They beckon us to move beyond dualistic thinking, urging us to perceive a deeper, interconnected reality.

In embracing these ideas, we begin to see the world through a lens that reveals the fabric of existence, where every thread is woven with purpose and meaning. **Synchronicity speaks to the moments of weighty coincidence that feel orchestrated by a higher intelligence, guiding us towards our true path.** Entangled mutuality reflects the discoveries of Quantum Mechanics as the interconnectedness of all beings, reminding us that our actions and thoughts reverberate through the collective consciousness, influencing and shaping the world around us.

To further illuminate this perspective, we will now turn our attention to the Lanka's science of psychology, examining its structure of human consciousness. By understanding this framework, we can gain deeper insights into the nature of our own minds and the greater reality we are a part of. Through this exploration, we hope to uncover the timeless wisdom that lies at the heart of human existence, offering a pathway to greater self-awareness and fulfilment.

Lanka: Chapter 6, section LXXXVI

What is judged good and evil is only due to the eight channels of consciousness.

They are the subconscious, the mind of objective thought, the attached mind of subjective will and discrimination, and the five senses of sight, hearing, smell, taste, and touch.

D.T. Suzuki, Introduction psychology

The Lanka offers a unique lens to understand psychology, viewing it through eight distinct functional areas or channels. Each of the five senses is perceived as an independent consciousness, capable of judgment and reaction.

The subconscious mind, often the source of what we perceive as consciousness, plays a crucial role. It collects experience impressions and feeds this subliminal information into the subjective mind *which then judges the sensory input within this context.*

The subjective mind, while providing the will and judgment, also has its pitfalls. It directs our thoughts and habitual reactions, **but in its creation of identity from the outcomes of thought, it can lead to an obsessive attachment. This attachment often outweighs its discernment, leading to unaware habitual responses, compulsive reactions, and defensive ego presentations.** *By understanding these potential pitfalls, we can navigate our own minds more effectively.*

The last functional area is the objective mind, which analyses and calculates, managing knowledge and rational discrimination.

Illusion, OWM

Some say the world is illusion spun, yet as it stands, it's quite real for everyone. Our perception, they claim, the illusory art, for the world is our creation, Mind-only at heart.

Mind crafted illusion, a veiled grand design, Some say thought is delusion, yet like reality, it's fine. **The delusion is believing we are those thoughts, and their outcomes, the world, in knots.**

Quiet the mind, let the turmoil cease, the world and thought, neither illusion nor decease. Without preferences, prejudice, or judgment to cloud, It just is, a truth simple yet loud.

Ancestors saw through, past misdirection's veil, rationality controlled, they set their sail. Once upon a time, wisdom's light shone bright, guiding through delusion, into the clear of night.

Lanka: Chapter 2, section IX

Why do the senses dominate waking consciousness?

*1. **We ignore our internal world for the external world,** viewing it as the sole reality that shapes our existence.*

*2. Consider how we often find ourselves **clinging to the external world,** to form and thought, driven by habit, insecurity, and fear.*

*3. **We protect our self-created identity through likes, dislikes, opinions, and beliefs.***

*4. **Infatuated with experience and its variety of pleasures,** we hold it dearly.*

Sense consciousness emerges in every sense organ, including its atoms, molecules, cells, and structures. Even the pores of the skin experience the sense field, sharing their entangled mutuality with every cell of the body.

However, the eye cannot see itself, nor can the finger touch itself. So, awareness is always the reflection of sense perception as seen against the subconscious and subjective mind. **Therefore, the action, the cause, and the experience are indistinguishably muddled unless stillness or suchness is achieved.**

Along with the senses, there is also an aspect of mind, the thinking function of consciousness, which may distinguish the objective world with distinct clarity. From this thinking mind comes the structure of life and the ability to control compulsiveness.

But this thinking mind and sense-consciousness generally have no idea that their parts are mutually and intimately conditioned to deceive each other, that **Mind-only projections are only representations of what is actual, not reality itself.**

Perception begins with preference, then thought, memory, and emotion. These are created primarily from subconscious collections, the imprints of action and consequence (karma). They include informed patterns of experience, inherited instinct and intuition. But the perception of reality is colored and created from a menagerie of randomly interconnected images, sound bites and programmed beliefs.

Slokas

100. **The collective subconscious (Alaya) is stirred by the winds of objectivity and creates consciousness in multiplicity.**

101. Dark blue, red, salt, the sound of the conch, milk, honey, fragrances, and rays of sunlight.

102. They are neither different nor the same, the ocean and its waves. This is how the sense-consciousness is connected to the absolute mind (Citta).

*103. **As waves are stirred in the ocean, the individual consciousness is created from the field of life .***

104. Absolute Mind, discerning mind, and consciousness consider the significance of each circumstance, but no part functions separately from another, as they lack independent character.

110. The apparent world is presented as such to our sense consciousness. Memory only appears to change. It is impermanent, reflecting the subconscious accumulation which changes like the waves.

*111. The ocean is seen dancing in waveness. **How is it that the intellect does not recognize collection in the living field?***

116. Because circumstances vary, the levels of delusion in awareness differ by degrees. The function of will and discrimination is to recognize an impersonal world while the discerning mind reflects upon its objective significance.

*117. While the physical world offers itself to the five senses, the one dwelling in Right-knowledge and remembrance of the true self is unperturbed. **There is little need for classification, comparison, and measurement where intuitive mindfulness abides instead of cascading thought.***

Waveness, **OWM**

Thou art energy, pure vibration, feeling life in mutual relation. **Elemental whispers in every part, organic, energetic brew, thou art.**

Radiating from thy form, so bright, entanglements of copious light.
Formless soup of existence's gleam, communicating, sustaining, creating the dream.

Following tides, by currents drawn, dancing in waveness, dusk till dawn.
Upon the ocean of existence brave, in essence true, thou art the wave.

Lanka: D.T. Suzuki, Relation of Functions

As the mind determines reality, it is a double-headed monster. One face peers into the subconscious, while without awareness, the other scans the sense consciousness to see countless things and hold them as real or unreal. They do not grasp the innate power of the subconscious field. Clinging to the outcomes of thought, they are caught in circumstance.

Here, we can say desire is the mother of compulsion and ignorance the father. But the mind is also a double-edged sword. When turning back occurs in the depths of one's subconscious, the arrangement changes in dramatic ways. **With one swing of the sword, duality is cut asunder, and the subconscious field is seen in its native purity as the solitary reality, free from discrimination or belief.**

Awareness, OWM

I am only this awareness, though a million things may disrupt, Not this body, until pain brings me to the ground abrupt.

Not this mind, until words misused spark debate, Not these thoughts, until identities' buttons activate. Nor compulsive reaction am I, until the tiger appearances threat, Truth disturbs collections my investment set.

I am only this awareness, when mind is still and body free, thoughts in meditation, subconscious may quietly see. Only this awareness, between thoughts, needs, and drives. Only this awareness, where pure seeing thrives. Not-two, not-knowing, no need for knowing's quest, To observe and listen wholly is this awareness quest. In still nature's mind, suchness shines clear, only this awareness removes subconscious fears.

Truth, in this way, reshapes thought's design, loving kindness boundless, beyond self interest define. Mind-only, creating, healing, shifting my being, healing in awareness, no prejudice of seeing,

Beyond outcomes, seeking highest good above all, devotion to truth and compassion heeds its call. **Freedom in awareness, joy beyond preference's chain, compassion replaces judgment, leaving no space for pain.**

No room for insult, resentment, or fear, awakening awareness, body, mind, and thoughts disappear. Listening, living intelligence profound, beyond right and wrong, awareness unbound.

Present here and now, awareness true, seeing I am not thoughts' outcomes, awareness full view. Free from compulsion, beliefs, and preference's snare, free from judgment is truth's beautiful flare.

Not creation, nor conception, just this awareness pure, in this space of being, I find my cure. In the silence of being, truth unfolds, emptiness and form, a tale retold.

Life's heartbeat a dance of light and shade, infinite connections, where all ending is remade.

As we finish Chapter Nine, we are reminded of the wisdom embedded in the ancient teachings of the *Lanka.* **The structures of mind, with their interplay**

of senses, thoughts, and subconscious influences, form the very fabric of our perceived reality.

By understanding these elements, we gain the power to transcend the limitations of habitual thought and sensory attachment, moving towards a state of pure awareness one could call enlightenment. This journey invites us to see beyond dualistic perceptions, embracing a deeper, interconnected reality where the self is no longer confined by ego or desire.

In embracing suchness and loving-kindness, we find the path to true freedom and peace, **recognizing that we are not merely the sum of our thoughts and experiences, but a part of the living, intelligent fabric of the universe.**

CHAPTER TEN
The Cosmology of Oneness

In the play of existence, the dance between form and formlessness reveals disarming truths about our reality and consciousness. **This chapter explores the coherence of ancient wisdom and modern science to unravel the nature of our interconnected universe.** From the Lanka's teachings, we learn that what we perceive as separate forms are intrinsically linked to the formless essence of existence. We invite you to journey beyond the illusions of individuality and duality, into a deeper understanding of the boundless and interwoven fabric of life.

Lanka: **Sagathakam, sloka**

*732. If form is to be found in the oneness of formlessness, it is not visible. **Its apparent non-existence contradicts the truth, though there is neither mechanism nor operator.***

Lanka: **Chapter 2, section XII**

***Rational men**, in their pursuit of understanding, often **focus on what may be observed in existence such as form, cause, effect, and interactions.** They may not account for the intricacies of space, seeing it as separate from form, and envisioning their separate lives. **However, the truth is that space is form, and as space permeates form, form is space.** In attempting to define these characteristics, we may consider the two as separate, but as form evolves, it becomes clear that it is not separate from space, as space exists abundantly within the form. This interplay of form and space, of observation and existence, is a fascinating aspect of our reality.*

When completely magnified and analyzed, the atom has no substance that can be found. *Though without static actuality, atoms are also not imaginary, and so only the concept or belief in matter remains. We cannot determine their existence or non-existence, as impermanence is valid for all things made of atoms.* **How then, may we argue what is or isn't real because the imagined may be just as natural as the stone, depending on its position in the cycle of impermanence we call time?** *This argument applies equally to ego perception, showing its insubstantiality as only a concept in time.*

The analytically minded see distinctions regarding atoms, elements, molecules, structure, and valences. They are attached to the notion that imaginary things are non-existent and assert that those things seen and experienced are real.

However, the accomplished scientist, in their pursuit of truth, understands that appearances are not always conclusive in determining what may seem imaginary, even if accepted by mutual reference. **The wisest among us do not accept the reality of what is seen and experienced at face value.** *They recognize that even the most rigorous analysis, going to the subtlest atomic particle, finds its state existing between being and non-being, or between reality and imagination.* **What can be measured are only characteristics that demonstrate a theory or idea of reality.** *This realization humbles us, reminding us of the limitations of our perception and the vastness of the unknown.*

Lanka: **Chapter 3, Section LXXV**

That which is not available for measurement is not expressible in words. *The inexpressible is said to be unborn without beginning or subject to destruction.*

That which is without beginning and not subject to destruction is like space, lacking cause and effect. **It is, therefore, unconditioned for understanding.** *As the rational mind does not fathom infinite space, so is the unknowable. In this way, the one seeking the absolute is likewise beyond understanding through the senses and their measurement.*

Clear, OWM

I think therefore I am, they say, yet not this body, mind, or thought's array. Not outcomes of knowledge or mind's grand design, I am this awareness, pure and divine.

Thou art that, beyond your knowing's reach, in formless infinity, your essence does breach. Thou thinkest and confuse yourself with outcomes' game, in this boundless expanse, thou art the same.

Existing as concept, I gather and define, yet it is not me, in formlessness, we intertwine. **Where does my concept end, and yours begin? Could it be there's only one of us within?**

In this vast expanse, where thoughts dissolve, awareness remains, the ultimate resolve. Not separate, but one, in this boundless sphere, only this awareness, forever clear.

Lanka: Sagathakam, slokas

127. The macroscopic and subatomic are bound together in mutual interchange. **Where life is determined, it is among elemental particles, and where elemental particles are seen, there is also life.**

128. Looking into the heart of an atom, no form can be judged as this or that. **What is confirmed is the truth of conscious projection or Mind-only, which cannot be grasped with ordinary thinking.**

129. This understanding does not belong to the scientific materialist or their students; it is experienced directly by awakening.

Particles, from the tiniest electrons to the swiftest photons, reveal a simple truth: they change when observed, showing that life is woven into the very fabric of existence. **Energy itself, as the ancient wisdom of the *Lanka* suggests, is alive.** This living energy is evident in the Observer Effect and the fascinating phenomenon of Quantum Entanglement.

The science of the *Lanka* speaks of a reality where nothing is separate. Life is a shared experience, a dance of entangled energies. To understand this, we must first recognize the ubiquitous life in energy and elements. **Imagine a world where every moment is a harmonious blend of space and time, where each cell in our bodies acts and reacts in perfect synchronicity with every other cell.**

Like a hologram, each cell contains the image of the whole. We are not isolated beings but integral parts of a magnificent, interconnected universe. **What may seem like a wild theory in our individual existence, is a fact verified within all the unanswered questions between physics, biology, and metaphysics.** Nothing is lost to embrace this vision and see how we are all part of life's grand, unified dance and there's everything to gain.

Lanka: **Chapter 3, section LXXIX**

Impermanence that exists in actuality and imagination is seen in those things made of elements, which in this context refer to the fundamental building blocks of matter. *These elements exist only in a constant flow of change and apparent destruction.* Things made of these elements have no *constancy or substantiality one may possess, but the elements themselves never change.*

Impermanence, the most fundamental non-dual force of nature, is alluded to as no-birth, no-destruction. *The atom, a mere idea, and form, a constant change, seems to exist statically. This is the unseen, the unborn, beyond modification, yet constantly fluctuating with thought.* **The ever-changing dependence on thought is the limitation and gift of impermanence, inviting us to experience the non-dual.**

Impermanence is universal in form, seen in the three divisions of time, past, present, and future. It is obscured in past time as forms and memory pass away. Its future is unborn and so unknown, while the present is mixed and muddled with the confusion of physical existence. **But when the atom is examined, there is no destruction, only recombination and changes in appearance.**

One might argue this last point in light of nuclear fission, but then *the Lanka*, from two thousand years ago is correct at the level of subatomic particle.

Boundless, OWM

An ecosystem is your wondrous frame, trillions of lives compose this wondrous game. **Worlds within worlds collide, where no electron is uniquely tied.**

Flowing, dancing, to and fro, resonating they come, resonating they go. One with all, in life we blend, aspects of energy without end.

Thou art resonance, waves of light, energy observed, particles in flight.

Through space you move, a trail you weave, atoms, energy, vibrations you leave.

Gathering all, you embody, absorb, this transient form, with no strict accord.

No start, no end in space confined, unseen, with others intertwined.

Infinitely small, infinitely grand, all things penetration you understand. **Part of everything, everything part of you, in full awareness, boundaries undo.**

Thou art boundless, free and whole, an infinite endless, interconnected soul.

Lanka: D.T. Suzuki*:* Introduction

*The concept of 'subconscious purity' is pivotal in our understanding of awakening. **It is the archive of all things, both good and bad, pure and defiled, yet its original nature remains pure and immaculately clean.** In our individual experiences of action and consequence (karma), this purity becomes soiled, as it indiscriminately collects all sensations, thoughts, concepts, and feelings. **This collection, while a normal sentient experience, can hinder intuitive insight**, leading us to follow beliefs created by imagination, superstition, domestication by others, or the ego-self. This identification confines us to the six realms of existence, known as actuality in limited sense-consciousness.*

*However, **the intuitive piercing of one's primitive subconscious purity is a catalyst for a revolution at all levels of consciousness,** leading to unification with the subconscious. So, our transformation or awakening would be impossible except for this puzzling concoction of pure and unclean, good and evil. Without this crucial step, we would remain trapped in relative duality, unable to step beyond our sentient animal existence.*

Turning back** is not just a mental aversion from unconscious, habitual, mundane life and its suffering. It **is a profound, direct experience that must be grasped with immediacy, experienced intimately, and penetrated

intuitively. This is the true objective of meditation and practice, and it demands our full commitment and engagement.

Noble Wisdom resides within the all-conserving subconscious. ***The collective subconscious, known as Alaya, may seem elusive and beyond psychological analysis, but it is within our reach.*** *Alaya exists at a pristine level, which can be accessed through suchness (non-conceptual awareness). Turning back, therefore, is a purification of subconscious access,* ***that can be achieved by relinquishing our infatuation with sensory indulgence, excessive material possessions, and the drama of obsessive thought.***

This restraint or stillness allows the perception of our oneness and allness.

Lanka: D.T. Suzuki, Introduction

Alaya is not a consciousness; it does not discern, judge, comprehend, or react. *As the collective subconscious, it is a neutral or a non-dual force within nature, which imprints and stores the resonance of action, consequence, experience, thought, and instinct for every life form within and outside their bodies.*

Lanka: Sagathakam, sloka

217. ***The collective subconscious field (Alaya), comes from our own bodies.*** *Then the individual's will claims a reality, based on its imprinted messages, according to likes and dislikes. The mind mistakenly interprets this as objective reality, coming from the outside in; without understanding this reality is only what we ourselves have created.*

Here, the *Lanka* voices the rigors of its ancient analytical science, which came as a complete surprise to me. **If the living energetic field (Alaya) is released from our bodies as entangled resonant energy, it must also be seen in respiration**, the sextillion particles making up each breath we exhale.

Interestingly, these particles of respiration are said to encircle the earth in a matter of days, shared by everyone on the planet as entangled living energy on a continual basis. The math also says, each breath we take contains particles or molecules from every other living thing having ever existed. **This would imply a degree of entanglement accounting for the living intelligence alluded to.**

The mind, guided by the senses, determines its actions and reactions. Yet, it is the subliminal input from the subconscious, both individual and collective, that provides the nourishment for these choices. **Dispersed in myriad energetic forms, these potential resources of unchanging knowledge are the very essence of our creative reflections.**

The Endless Array, OWM

Countless particles shift and dance, in waves unseen, they find their chance. Observed, they form a measured beam, where synchrony is lost within the stream.

One shift, all shift, distance defied, time and space, now cast aside. Synchronicity glows as energy's spread, in life's entanglement, we're each its thread.

We see form and DNA's trace, yet it's vibration that holds it all in place. Not-separate, completely intertwined, within ourselves, are all humankind.

Unchanging knowledge, effortless flow, one thing in many places glow. Access to all, if we but hear, the whisper of truth, ever near.

How far from synchrony this reality? The starling's dance, its vast mystery. Migrations timed with perfect grace, weather's call from a distant place.

More mysterious still, this human form, balance within, cells and microbes swarm. **Vast symbiosis, an entangled whole, one being, one life, the vehicle of soul.**

No barriers of space and time, one life-force connected within the clime. The mutual expression, life's grand play, thou art the wave, in endless array. **Energy entangled, space in between, oneness and allness, unseen. Thou art the pulse, the cosmic rhyme, thou art eternal, beyond time.**

Lanka: **Chapter 3, Section LXXVIII, slokas**

108. Original nature is only to be recognized in its complete interdependence, not as fantasy or unreality. ***All things and life arise in sequence and continuity, dependent and interlocking strings of causation.***

109. In this connection, called no-birth or concatenation, the essence of all things are seen with new eyes, as indivisible.

110. ***When the concatenation is clear, the mind acquires peace****.*

111. ***Personality, ego, desire and karma are only inward facing concatenations****. The outward facing concatenations, also strings of interdependence, are physical reality, materials, creations, and living things, etc.*

112. This is the law of nature, as all things are interdependently co-arising in the mutuality of entangled energy, expressed as form, life and knowledge.

Lanka: **Sagathakam, sloka**

*96. Suspending the notion of cause and conditional control, is to be free of causal excuses leading to **the recognition of Mind-only—this is the state of*** *full responsibility called no-birth as a non-dual law of nature.*

Lanka: Chapter 2, Section XXVII

*As to the meaning of non-duality, it means that all terms of opposites (duality) are relative in nature and do not exist independently from one another. There is no darkness without light to define it. There is no short without long to define it. There is no hell without heaven to define it. Pleasure only exists relative to pain. **Therefore, the wise understand the non-dual nature of appearance as empty of independent existence, devoid of substance or original nature.** This is called no-birth, and no-self-nature in the ancient terms, which alludes to its immutability.*

Lanka: Chapter 6, Section LXXXII

*The womb of enlightenment (Tathagatagarbha) or subconscious is the cause for both good and evil throughout all forms and circumstances. Like an actor playing a roll, it functions without conscience nor thought for consequences, as it lacks consciousness. But **the living energy surrounding and infusing our planet is our great ocean of existence, which is not changed at depth by our minor waves of interaction.** This living field (Alaya) remains pure in its essential nature which includes all life for all time.*

Here Quantum Physics offers plausibility beyond metaphysics because this field is plausible by entangled mutuality or the time-space synchronicity of living things.

Life's Whole, OWM

No judgment of right or wrong, no thoughts of good or bad belong. The tiger slays to feed its young, A timeless song, in nature sung.

Thou art the tiger, fierce and bold, The deer, whose life's tale is told.

The cub, in innocence, unaware, in this dance of life, thou art there.

Non-dual essence, a caring whole, life's symphony, nature's unified soul. Loving beyond mere self and its claim, in this boundless love, all value the same.

Thou art life without confines, flowing through all eternal lines. Impermanence, life's grand design, observed beyond duality's sign.

Thou art that, the endless weave, of existence's fabric, never to leave.

Commingling all, in oneness found, in every heartbeat, nature's sound.

Life observed, beyond the strife, in this oneness, to find true life. Thou art the wave, the ocean's crest, the eternal breath, in unity blessed.

Conclusion

Chapter Ten, reminds us that our essence transcends the physical and mental constructs we often cling to. The wisdom of oneness calls us to recognize the interconnectedness of all things, where each particle, thought, and experience is part of a greater whole.

In this awareness, we find freedom from the illusions of separation and limitation. Embracing the cosmology of oneness, we awaken to our true nature—boundless, interconnected, and in harmony with the entire universe. This understanding guides you towards a life of compassion, mindfulness, and empathetic connection with all that is.

CHAPTER ELEVEN
Suchness

In the journey toward higher understanding, this exploration forms a crucial passage. **The *Lanka* teachings, emphasize the significance of comprehending the relationship between knowledge and consciousness.**

Knowledge manifests in three distinct forms: worldly, spiritual, and transcendental. Worldly knowledge, shared by both the learned and the ordinary.

Spiritual knowledge transcends physical limitations, yet remains tethered to dualistic outcomes.

Transcendental knowledge moves beyond individual experiences, engaging with the non-dual. This chapter delves into these layers of knowledge, guiding us towards a realization of our inherent oneness with all existence.

Lanka: Chapter 3, Section LXVI

For those with the highest intention, it is crucial to comprehend the entangled relationship between knowledge and consciousness. Respectively defined as the awareness or understanding of facts, information, or skills, versus the state of being aware, perceiving and understanding one's surroundings in total clarity.

*Knowledge, as we know it, can be categorized into three types: worldly, spiritual, and transcendental. **Worldly knowledge, which is accessible to both the cultured and the common folk, can be likened to a state of slumber. It is oblivious to dimensions of being that extend beyond the physical and mental, thus limiting one's understanding to the material world we perceive.***

Spiritual knowledge, on the other hand, is a realm that the seeker, the student, and those enlightened of mind delve into. It is characterized by an awareness that transcends form and rationalization, guided by our innate intuitive consciousness. **Here, we begin to see beyond the limitations of physical existence. However, our understanding is still confined to the realm of personality, as the outcomes of thought and dualistic gain or loss.** *In this struggle, we often suffer, not fully grasping the immense power of our oneness or allness. For instance, a spiritual seeker might experience a deep sense of peace and unity during meditation, transcending the physical and mental realms, yet be sent to fits of rage in a traffic jam.*

Transcendental knowledge, not a product of thought but an experience of the primordial subconscious, *is born from engaging with the non-dual living intelligence of all life. It is an awareness and engagement with synchronicity, the mutuality of energetic entanglement or oneness. Beyond the confines of individuality, doing, achieving, and its inevitable decay, this supernatural knowledge is reinforced by direct experience.* **It is characterized by the perspective of imagelessness, sublime composure, and a harmony with all life, realizing inseparability.**

Perception, OWM

With each moment, a million stimuli cascade, eyes, nose, ears, taste, and touch invade. Only in quietude, the chaos may cease, perceiving one-one hundredth, finding inner peace.

In that perception, echoes resound, the wisdom of ancestors, profound and unbound. Gaia and all life, your lineage and guide, in your consciousness, their truths abide.

Thou art the combined wisdom, ageless and vast, a tapestry woven from the distant past. Unchanging knowledge, a light within, not found in the world, but where introspection begins.

Lanka: Sagathakam, sloka

270. *A theory or idea only establishes a possible source of reality;* **suchness is the natural state of a quiet mind, which grasped, gives the yogin certitude of Mind-only.**

This simple statement encapsulates the essence of various meditative practices such as mindfulness, emptiness, and Zazen. Ironically, suchness exists in every moment between every two thoughts. By pausing and listening intently, we can grasp its stillness and perceive the subconscious feelings available through intuition. This experience of suchness aligns with certitude, often recognized as the sixth stage of consciousness, representing a deeper, more intuitive understanding of reality.

Lanka: Chapter 6, section LXXXIII

Truth and faith (Dharma) are characterized by name, form, belief, right knowledge, and suchness which transcends thought. **Direct experience of the unchanging, called right knowledge, penetrates the formless essence of things.** *Here, the yogin enters the inner realization of suchness, where notions of dependence, purposelessness, realism, and negativity are of no consequence. Like this, he or she attains the seat of tranquillity in the world as it is. This tranquilization is called the correct acquisition of truth.*

Generally, men and women suffer the illusion of separation, dreaming that each thing is real in itself and that, what we think is who we are. **We** *need to understand that the illusion is seeing many, where there is only one.* Then, believing we are created by God, time, or atoms, we worship wealth, fame, and beauty, missing the fact that they are illusionary concepts that arise in a dreamlike fashion.

Right Knowledge is described as a transcendental understanding through direct experience of what is, as it is, instead of form, names, and beliefs, which are usually confused with static reality. These appearances are impermanent distinctions due to our mutual conditioning and complete interdependence.

Through the experience of the absolute, there is no more infatuation with thought, the world, or consciousness. **In this knowledge, reactions calm themselves, and senses are tranquilized in seeing the eternal nature of all things as constant change and commingling interdependence.**

When a perspective is attained rid of dualistic arguments, this is called 'suchness'. **In suchness, definitions of self by names and appearances dissolve. Suchness is a state of being where one sees things as they truly are without the distortions of preconception.** This progress is the road to imagelessness, and attained along the way is the stage of joyous composure.

Entering suchness, one doesn't just attain true freewill, but also a freedom that is devoid of compulsions and obsessions. This is not just a theoretical possibility, but a reflection of the evolution of awareness, free from obsessive will and desire with its thought-constructions.

Lanka: Sagathakam, slokas
154. The world, when seen without the veil of distortion, reveals a profound truth, the perceiver and the perceived are not separate entities. The world, as it is, is not the world as seen.

82

155. Habitually, memory and thought stir the mind to perceive an illusionary external world. **When this habit ceases to control, our innate, ever-present knowledge replaces it.** *This understanding, intuitive wisdom, and suchness are unconstrained by appearances because they lay beyond thought.*

156. Form, name, and judgment correspond to worldly knowledge, whereas **Right Knowledge and Suchness correspond to perfected wisdom.**

Suchness, OWM

Thou art the mind's quiet center, where no disturbance dares to enter. Your true nature, effortlessly revealed, ineffable, unflappable, peacefully sealed.

Comprehend this one thing, sit and rest, striving ceases in harmony's quest.

Center of the universe, creator of all, reconciling worlds with love's gentle call.

Not Larry or Sue, not Mom or Dad, not master or slave, identities clad.

Center of the cyclone, quiet eye of being, peace profound, beyond all seeing.

This suchness, the mind's fundamental part, In stillness and quiet, thou art.

Tat twam asi! Thou art that, in the depths of your soul, where true peace is at.

Lanka : Chapter 2, Section IX(a)

Within the realm of Noble Wisdom, there exist three philosophical aspects: the enigmatic concept of imagelessness, the transformative power bestowed by awakened beings, and the ultimate goal of self-realization.

Imagelessness arises in mastery of all paths; where identifications, attachments and questions have been thoroughly extinguished and mastered. It's a state where life **has lost all preponderance and spiritual vanity.**

*The aspect of noble wisdom called **transmission is a testament to the transcendental power of awakened beings.** These threads of energy are given to take root and accelerate growth. It's a guiding force that leads the open heart, focused mind, and discerning eye to see.*

__Self-realization is the state where the guileless heart perceives all things in their nonmaterial essence rather than as mere phenomena.__ It's a state where the meditative consciousness reveals both suffering and self to be illusory creations of the mind. __In this state, delight in the world 'as it is', becomes the blissful common thread of life and creative expression.__

The fugue, OWM

What I do to others, I do to myself, what I do for others, I do for myself. What I do to myself, I do to everyone, what I do for myself, I do for everyone.

This is the circle thou art, entwined, in actions and deeds, in heart and mind.

When you lie, thou art deceived, when you give, thou receiveth.

When you steal, thou art robbed, when you love all others, thou art loved.

To love fully, with a guileless heart, most dearly beloved, is truly your part.

A mystery of discernment applied, you cannot see but what you are inside. Not seeing guile, thou art free of guile, not seeing separateness, acceptance is your smile.

All you see is mind's reflection, joy being thus your true expression, loving-kindness, wisdom's gift bestowed, The guileless heart, intuitively known.

Exhausting separateness, love takes its place, acceptance and kindness, is human grace. In this circle of being, we find our art, one and all, within the unified heart.

Lanka: **Chapter Two, Section LVI**

Begin the journey of self-discovery by withdrawing from the external world and delving into the depths of your being. **Relying solely on your own intellect and will, strive to rid yourself of misguided attitudes and beliefs.**

How does one navigate this great way? Are there not countless paths to explore within oneself?

There exists a path, a path that only a few may comprehend. This path reveals itself when belief, especially the belief of being the doer, dissipates. **In this state of 'not doing' and 'not believing, 'the essence of suchness unveils the great way. Nothing is left undone,** *so the 'doer' assumes a functional significance only. In the absence of clinging, everything unfolds in the harmony and synchronicity of interdependent co-arising.*

Lanka: **Chapter Two, Section XXIII**

The three natural dispositions of the mind are belief or false discrimination, knowledge of relativity, and innate knowledge. **False discrimination arises from infatuation with form and belief in physical reality.** *This delusion is called attachment to names and forms. Knowledge of relativity (duality) arises from belief in the separation of subject and object. This confusion is the dividing nature of discrimination.*

Innate knowledge is available beyond the first two dispositions. We find it focusing on intuition and realizing the self, not as form, subject, or object.

Thus, carrying no labels or self-images, we reside in non-cognitive awareness, mindfulness as suchness.

Lanka: **Chapter Two, Section XXXVII**

What is this meditation that suchness is its objective? **When Yogins encounter imagelessness, the loss of identification or attachment to personality, they recognize life and death as imaginative veils.** *When they are grounded in this intuitive state of being, belief, judgment, and opinion, cease to obscure their vision. This way of being is the meditation with suchness as its outcome.*

Lanka: Chapter 3, Section LXXIX

The three worlds, desire, form, and formlessness (thought), are taught as the projection of the mind itself. Everything and everyone else is recognized to be dependent on each other and arising together. **This relationship is understood as the foundation of oneness, to disregard the dualistic nature of an independent existence.**

When one understands one's role as co-creator, lessons to be learned or experienced do not require judgment or drama, as their temporary and frivolous nature is obvious. We can simply accept a mistake or lesson and move on. **In this way, comparisons become less important, as Mind-only is understood through direct experience.**

Freedom also occurs as an attachment to outcomes, loses its power. **When external things are no longer invested with sovereignty or seen as separate, misidentification and the burdensome practice of judging disappear.** *Here, faith in life itself, replaces the fear and stress of unfulfilled desires. When this practice of subject/object transcendence is recognized, there is no question of 'what is?' nor 'What is not?' Mind-only is actualized.*

But we are no less alive and engaged because judgment still arises from work's intention and one's self-worth as a creative person. **When delusion ceases, the discrimination or judgment of the three worlds is just the** *outcome of words,* *with no greater value than temporary usefulness.*

The Oneness, OWM

Reimagine life's heartbeat grand design, alive, aware, energy life-force intwined. Observing waves, they morph to particles' might, waveness dissolving in space boundless flight.

Energy and vibration, immeasurable and free, observe the mind's dance from wave to particle, see. Life, fleeting, emerges from emptiness' core, returns to emptiness, the cycle evermore.

Emptiness as wave, awareness and reaction, a field of interconnection, no part, no fraction. Interdependent co-arising, mutual and whole, linked in entangled dependencies, might call it the soul.

Thou art Gaia's corpuscle, in starlight's moonbeam, every pulse, every atom, every part of life's dream.

Lanka: Chapter 3, Section LXII, sloka

*10. **When identification with physical reality is seen for its illusion, cause disappears into the comingling of life, and there is no sense of obligation, blame, or guilt.** Intuitive awareness supersedes certainty of belief, opinion, and judgment. This awareness is the nature of suchness, the domain of spiritual wisdom.*

Conclusion

In the quiet sanctuary of the mind, free from the ceaseless chatter of judgment and the burdens of duality, lies the essence of suchness. This state of being transcends the dichotomies of right and wrong, good and bad, reflecting the natural order of the universe where all forms of life, from the tiger to the deer to the cub, are interconnected. **Suchness invites us to embrace impermanence, recognizing life's transient nature while understanding our integral role within the mindfulness of existence.** It is here, in the stillness between thoughts, that we discover the unchanging knowledge, the effortless belonging that connects us to the divine. In this awareness, we see beyond physical forms and labels, experiencing life as a harmonious flow of energy and consciousness. **By letting go of outcomes and embracing the synchronicity of interdependent co-arising, we attain true freedom.**

This chapter reveals that suchness is not just a concept but a lived reality, a path to awakening where love, joy, and compassion replace fear and separation. **Through this thorough realization, we align ourselves with the ultimate truth of being—thou art that.**

CHAPTER TWELVE
Psychology

In the tangled maze of consciousness, understanding the nature of our mind is pivotal. This chapter delves into the insights as interpreted by D.T. Suzuki, on the psychology of consciousness.

At its core, consciousness is the capacity to discern, comprehend, and react to the world around us. Each of the five senses—sight, sound, smell, taste, and touch—along with thought, forms the foundation of our perception. **Yet, beyond this sensory engagement lies the subjective mind, which constructs and defends our identity from infancy, often trapping us in habitual patterns and illusions.** This identification with thought fosters a dualistic view, where we mistake the transient world of forms as the ultimate reality.

By exploring these layers of consciousness, we embark on a journey to transcend the compulsive subjectivity that blinds us, moving towards true self-realization and the freedom of a quiet mind. **This journey is not just about understanding but about self-discovery, about peeling back the layers of our conditioning to reveal our true selves.**

Lanka: D.T. Suzuki, Psychology

Consciousness, as a higher function of life, only means to discern, comprehend, and possibly react. So, in seeing, we distinguish between a red apple or white cloth, which is eye-consciousness. Sound, smell, taste, feeling, and thought are experienced similarly.

Each consciousness can perceive and react independently. We comprehend the world externally and internally through these five forms of sense consciousness and thought.

Identity with thought, or subjective consciousness, is the most important organ of thought. In its natural state, characterized by will and judgment, constructing and defending identity was its first job from birth and remains its priority. The subjective mind not only drives thought and reflection, obsessed with the outcomes of thinking as self, but it lives in habitual addiction.

Oblivious to the workings of consciousness, we react out of habituated patterns of thought, belief, and behavior. **This is sleepwalking through life, where the natural identification of self with the outcome of thought creates the clinging to the dualistic world as the only reality.**

We should all understand sleepwalking through life, is the loss of free will. But it starts naturally with the construction of sense consciousness as part of animal evolution.

Yet, rational thought finds itself in a constant struggle, subordinated to an insecure identification that takes root in infancy and solidifies in childhood. **Until this identity crisis is resolved, the cage of compulsive subjectivity remains locked, and the free will of objective discernment becomes a fleeting, distant idea.**

Lanka: **Chapter 7, section LXXXIX**

The seven channels of sense-consciousness are thought, the attached mind, and the five senses (sight, smell, hearing, touch, taste), which are characterized by their temporary and habitual nature. **Active sense consciousness lacks sufficient merit to facilitate transformation. Its collections and functions do not define self nor pass beyond death.**

Reincarnation reflects only the subconscious, which is also the gateway of nirvana or pleasure and pain.

*Like the craftsman dependent on materials and tools, transformation is a craft of slow change. Transformation is taught as it plays to the audience's need and their capacity for understanding. **Doctrine's purpose is to provide progress and relief of suffering, but it is not the whole truth, which words can never contain.** Truth arises in self-realization, experienced as not-separate oneness.*

Foolish people think of death or the end of sense-conscious as meaninglessness because they fail to understand their subconscious self. So, they dream of heaven and hell. Their dream is eternal life for the ego-personality, oblivious to belief's limits.

***Actual freedom begins as belief itself is discarded.** Addictive routines can only then be recognized to address the habits of self-centered delusion, obsessive desire, greed, and intellectual pride.*

Limitation, OWM

Formless awareness, discrimination dismissed, waking sleep, self as thought persists. Trails of outcome color what is, masks of good, bad, or irrelevant quiz.

Self-imposed personality, fiercely protected, ideas of self, by clinging, perfected.

Hungry for experience, excitement's flame, pleasure's feast, yet dissatisfaction's name. **What is this trap of sense-consciousness? A cycle of unending restlessness.**

Ascertain joy, examine peace within, thou art not this mind, nor body's skin. Not this collection, not this tale, bars of discrimination, where senses fail.

Sunset's colors missed, flowers unseen, life's fragrances lost in routine. Begin as one intends to carry on, gratitude's seed, in spirit, dawns.

Gratitude, a practice, generous and kind, not mere words, but deeds aligned. Giving, serving, with thought sincere, generosity of spirit, crystal clear.

Peace, the guileless heart's embrace, magic in listening, a giving grace.

Thou art joy, to love, always free, in blessed emptiness, acceptance, decree.

The cage, not locked, thou art free, in faith and love, eternally.

Lanka: Chapter 2, Section LIII

Identifying oneself with the outcomes of thought, the world of things *appears as the only reality to the subjective mind. Through habit and memory, it nourishes the subconscious mind and programs the objective mind to which it clings and protects. Though without physicality or characteristics, the disturbed subconscious is both the cause and support of sense consciousness.* **Mutually conditioned life evolves and dissolves, but when the subjective mind rids itself of willing and judging, the fabric of control ceases.** *So, it is said:*

179. I do not find Nirvana through being, practice, work, or recognition. I enter its non-dual awareness beyond discrimination when preferences, opinions, beliefs, and judgments cease.

Lanka: Chapter 2, Section XXIV

Habitual thought and the belief in separateness see existence changing continually, like a river or clouds in the sky; *like a monkey mind, always* *restless, indiscriminately feeding; like a fly searching for unclean things and defiled places, it is never satisfied.*

So, life goes on reanimating dead beliefs, memories, and experiences in an endless cycle of compulsive consumption and unconscious fantasy.

By compassionately understanding these tendencies, one bears witness to the typical patterns of life and the insubstantiality of ego identification. This perspective of our own selves and others, is grasping our oneness.

Lanka: Chapter 2, Section XV

The illusion that reality exists separate from one's own projection creates false imagination, enumerable flaws, frauds, and misrepresentations. These appear to be magically produced, but in truth, they are compulsions, infatuations, and identification with physical reality, as all there is.

Lanka: Chapter 2, section XLIX

The very essence of identity is a fluid concept, intricately woven in our habitual thoughts, illusions of personality, and disposition. It is a product of our sense limitations, existing in a perpetual state of change, devoid of any static reality, actuality, or fantasy. This fluidity is the wellspring of our understanding, constantly shaping and reshaping our perception of self.

Personality, a complex interplay of inborn tendencies and beliefs, is not a fixed entity. It is, in fact, a reflection of our awareness, a product of our imagination. This interplay between inheritance and thought construction is the very fabric of our self-perception, the imagination of who we believe ourselves to be.

Imagination does not become accurate with discriminating judgment; it is still only a mirage of our making. But in setting aside personality, clinging ceases, though nothing is lost. This discipline is to enter the stream of conscious evolution.

Though we can't think our way to awakening, there are three key tools that can guide us towards a deeper understanding. *The first is the ability to set aside our preconceived notions of personality. The second is the practice of questioning our projected reality. The third is the continuous pursuit of doing the next right thing.*

These tools can free us from the shackles of delusion by cutting the knots of materiality that bind us. *When these knots are finally broken, the negative emotions of coveting, anger, fear, and folly dissipate.*

Conclusion

As we conclude this exploration of consciousness, **we recognize that our habitual thoughts and beliefs shape our perception of reality, often leading to a cycle of compulsive behavior and self-deception.**

The *Lanka* teachings guide us towards a sudden awakening, where the illusions of separateness and ego dissolve. In this state of suchness, we experience life as an interconnected flow, free from the distortions of dualistic thinking. By embracing the tools of awakening, setting aside personality, questioning projected realities, and continually striving to do the right thing, we break free from the knots of delusion.

This chapter reveals that true freedom lies in transcending the habitual mind, experiencing life with an intuitive understanding that sees beyond the physical and embraces the oneness of all existence. In this awakened state, we find peace, joy, and a deeper connection with the world, realizing that our true nature is boundless and interconnected with all that is.

CHAPTER THIRTEEN
Self-Realization

Embarking on the journey of self-realization is to navigate the depths of our own consciousness, shedding the layers of illusion and ego that obscure our true nature. The remainder of this book is about the reflection of transcendental knowledge as taught in the *Lanka*.

This chapter explores the path towards self-realization, emphasizing the renunciation of ignorance and the embrace of meditative consciousness. Through disciplined practice, one transcends habitual thinking and enters a state of awakened wisdom, where discrimination and attachment cease. Here, the enlightened mind perceives reality with transcendental knowledge and compassion, recognizing the impermanent and illusory nature of all things.

Lanka: Chapter 2, section XVI

As one dismantles the belief in externality and comes to the realization of the Mind-only creation, the five aspects of sentient beings, appearances, ego, and subjective reality lose their grip and lift their veils, revealing insight into reality just as it is.

***Those renouncing ignorance at this stage of mental concentration, step into self-realization as the freedom of emptiness.** This path of meditative consciousness includes the correct acquisition of truth while still working on habitual thinking and their own cycles of transformation.*

Lanka: Chapter 3, section LXXIII

What is meant by the attainment of truth? It is the right understanding of self, a subtle function of mind, and the oneness or interdependence of all things, wherein prejudice ceases. **This understanding empowers us to perceive the stages of consciousness and a focused suchness to turn away from the compulsive mind.** *Self-centered thoughts and their willing, discriminating aspect of identification dwindle. Here, one enters the path of awakened wisdom and holds to selflessness.* **One becomes master of all things by letting go to oneness, in faith and loving kindness.** *Hence the attainment of truth means freedom from attachment to discrimination, dualistic notions and unsound reasoning.*

Lanka: Chapter 2, sloka

2. The enlightened mind sees all things through transcendental knowledge and compassion. **Like a fantasy, the perception is impermanent, illusory, and insubstantial, beyond the greatest intellect as it witnesses essence.** *Understanding this perception is beyond being and non-being, so it has no substance for the mind to grasp.*

Lanka: Chapter 2, Section VII

The guileless seekers (Bodhisattvas) will soon understand that the world of bliss and the world of sorrow are one. **This perspective will show in their tranquillity, as loving actions cleverly devise means of helping others to awaken.** *Because they see beyond physical cause, everything arises effortlessly, untouched by the Mind's creation through meditative consciousness and interdependent entanglement. Here, progress in understanding the triple world of desire, form, and formlessness is assured.*

These highest seekers penetrate the state of imagelessness, recognizing the truth of Mind-only with perfected discipline, in which there is no thought of self or the attachment to doing. Attuned to the transformations of suchness, its freedom is their bliss.

In the turning back within the subconscious, they may also realize paranormal and clairvoyant gifts, as well as self-control, love, compassion and the ability to apply one's gifts appropriately. **All that is necessary for life is provided in this great attainment by the living field of life (Alaya)** *beyond memory, thinking, and the previously beholden self.*

Lanka: Chapter Four, Section LXXX

At the sixth stage (self-nature of certitude), the selfless seekers attain perfect tranquilization. *However, for a variety of renunciates and Buddhas of other paths, there is still engagement with life (karma) and dualism, having not attained a clear conviction of oneness or the end of discrimination. So, tranquilization for them is not continuous until the seventh stage (self-nature of Buddhahood).*

Awakening has many levels. **Only at the final stage do seekers end the love affair with ideas arising from memory, thought, and self-identified mind.** *However, from the first to sixth stages, one increasingly perceives the triple world of illusion as no more than stuck images and mistaken stories entangled with unhealthy feelings of identification.*

Renunciates and Buddhas enlightened from outside means, who reach the final level of selflessness will experience intoxicating peace, bliss, and happiness. *But this may become a trap if they fail to see that the world is only and always the creation of the mind. Habitually thinking of life and individuality, they may be caught in the notion of Nirvana or a life of magical happiness, which misses the truth of solitude as the expression of not-separate awareness.*

As selfless ones (Bodhisattvas) experience peace and tranquillity, their love and sympathy cultivate their character in service to others. Their path unfolds in certainty and faith, whereby all means to their work are provided in synchronicity through vows of devotion and surrender. **Usually perceived as magical blessings, effortlessness is experienced. Nirvana ceases as a goal because their life, without the agitation of discrimination, judgment, and opinion, is the experience of Nirvana itself.** Here, loss and gain are seen equally as nothing to grasp and no one grasping, only blessings and lessons in a path of growth. The world is observed as the mind itself, where belief is surrendered to the open listening of intuition and focused awareness.

A man sleeps and dreams, struggling to cross the great river. **Suddenly awakened, he asks, "Is this real, or is it imaginary?"** It is neither real nor make-believe, only the habit of memory and thinking bubbling from the mind, attached to discrimination and self-will.

Ultimate reality has no gradation of scale nor continuous character. It exists in neither time nor space. Absolute solitude is taught as its own truth, while images of discrimination and belief are seen as folly and naturally quieted. **What gradation can there be where imagelessness prevails?**

Lanka: Chapter 2, Section XXX

How does the advanced student regard the manifestations and struggles of life and death?

In oneness, there is no such thing as self, the other, or bothness. All things created are just notions of us and them, projections. The wise see both inner and outer concatenations as conforming to Mind-only, beyond predictability arising interdependently. **Here, they witness the dreamlike**

normality, transcending identification as the doer with the outcomes of thought.

Understanding the nature of reality, the natural dispositions, and the falsehood of separateness, they attain the power of will-body. **Regarding the notions of birth, life, and death as inconsequential, the usual limitations of body and mind cease to constrain them.**

Lanka: Chapter 8

A vegetarian diet is recommended for the highest attainment of those who follow the Buddhas. Planting roots of goodness, they possess faith and avoid discrimination, attachment, greed, and covetousness. **They see all men, women, and children as one's dearest family but without attachment.**

This compassion is the expression of Buddha nature, *wherein lies peace and joy to embrace all living beings with affection as our own person, and to regard all beings as if they were our only child.*

Awakening, OWM

Thou art that, awakening from the sleep of thought, truth lies beyond the mind, in a realm unbought. Right or wrong fades, it's all good and slight, In purposeless understanding, pure presence takes flight.

In the moment, agendas set aside, for the greatest good, let intuition guide. **Hold space fully, love subconscious deep, layers of separateness peel, revealing all we seek.**

Experience imagelessness, self uncovered and true, right-knowledge blooms in direct becoming's view. Self-obsession fades, outcomes let go, emptiness of self allows true knowledge to grow.

Emptiness forms the space for becoming's dance, not separate, oneness belongs at a glance. Thou art emptiness, yet fullness and all, in this truth, no greater ambition can call.

Embrace the allness, where ambitions cease, in the fullness of being, find ultimate peace.

Conclusion

The path to self-realization, as illuminated by *the Lanka*'s teachings, is a transformative journey that transcends the illusions of ego and separateness. As we progress through the stages of awakening, we increasingly perceive the world as a manifestation of mind, liberated from the confines of habitual thinking and dualistic notions. **At the highest levels of realization, the enlightened mind attains a state of tranquilization and effortlessness, where Nirvana is not a distant goal but a lived experience.** This chapter reveals that true self-realization lies in recognizing the interconnectedness of all existence, embracing a life of loving kindness, and surrendering to the flow of synchronicity. Through this journey, we find that the ultimate reality is beyond time, space, and discrimination, an undifferentiated state of pure awareness and compassion. **As we let go of self-centered thoughts and embrace our Buddha nature, we cultivate a life of peace, joy, and boundless generosity, witnessing the world as it truly is: a reflection of our own awakened mind.**

CHAPTER FOURTEEN
Difficult Questions

In the transcendental teachings of *the Lanka*, we are invited to transcend the illusions of judgment, ego, and the attachments that bind us to a false sense of self. Chapter Two, Section XXXV, illuminates the futility of clinging to the past and the illusion of separation that arises from it. **Just as the wind in the trees is indifferent to judgment or the past, we are encouraged to recognize the noise of a restless mind as mere distractions from our true nature.** Through the teachings of *the Lanka*, we learn to perceive the world beyond duality and ego, seeing the interdependent nature of all existence. This chapter explores the deep insights into the nature of ego-soul, the eternal-unthinkable creator, and the path to self-realization, offering a serious understanding of our interconnectedness and the ultimate truth of oneness.

Lanka: **Chapter Two, Section XXXV**

Like the wind in the trees, speaking of judgment or the past finds neither truth nor untruth. What cares the wind?

Us and them, real and unreal, come from old, scratched recordings or sound bites of memory. This is a foolish habit that increases the false notion that memories are worthy of confidence. It is just the noise of an uncontrolled mind pretending to be oneself.

Lanka: **Sagathakam, slokas**

757. Imagining celestial music, the masses seek an ego-soul within sense-consciousness.

758. As one seeks precious stones where they are visible, so do they seek a soul in the five aspects of sentient beings.

*759. But the mind cannot see its reasoning nor its functions connected by consciousness. **Not found, ego-soul within sense-consciousness is taken on faith to assume permanence.***

760. But as the womb is not seen by the woman who bears it, the ego-soul is not visible in sentient characteristics.

*761. Like the essence of medicine or the fire energy within kindling, **some deny the ego-soul within sense-consciousness out of loyalty to the path of emptiness.***

762. However, before enlightenment, one cannot find the essence of things in both permanence and emptiness, caught as they are in the identification with form, and thought. So, it is with ego-soul as an aspect of sentience.

*763. **However, without the ego-soul, we have no purpose in stages of development, self-mastery, clairvoyance, attainments, or the bliss of meditative consciousness.***

*764. **So, when the inquisitor comes to say, "Show me this ego-soul, if it exists," the sage would say, "show me your discrimination."***

Here the *Lanka* stands in what may be seen as a violation of Buddhist doctrine, while proving out the case that ego-soul is absolute mind in the aspect of subconscious. In understanding the physics of biological entanglement, **one might consider the life force in every cell as ego-soul, while simultaneously respecting Buddhism's no ego-soul for its wisdom, in that soul is not a function of sense-consciousness**. Continuation may be seen as a non-dual aspect of the subconscious, therefore beyond understanding.

Lanka: **Chapter 2, Section XVII**

The concept of an eternal unthinkable creator, *a notion that transcends the realm of rational thought, is profoundly intriguing. It defies the traditional understanding of cause and effect in creation, which is **often expressed in a dualistic manner, as a differentiated source or a separated being and its creation.** However, this duality is not applicable to the eternal or infinite, as the creator is non-dual and undifferentiated. This concept, therefore, lacks a causal connection, as no separation of creator and creation is possible. **In essence, creation itself is the eternal unthinkable creator, a notion that invites us to delve deeper into the mysteries of existence.***

*The eternal and unthinkable, much like space, exists as the preeminent reality of creation. It is not a distant concept, but something that can be experienced in the realization of one's absolute self, as not separate. **In this realization, the highest reality becomes its own causation, as there is no-doer.** This is the essence of suchness, a reality that can be actualized within each of us, inviting us to explore our deepest selves and subconscious minds.*

*As Buddha eloquently puts it, the eternal unthinkable is not a concept that can be confined to the realms of philosophy. **It is a unique and exalted state of self-realization, oneness where no other than self (not separate) is the highest reality.** It is a causation where there is no doer, a non-dual, space-like, nirvana-like, and discrimination-ending reality. It is the eternal, living intelligence of all life, a concept transcending the eternal unthinkable spoken in philosophy. It is the essence of thatness or suchness, a reality that can be realized by the Noble Wisdom within each of our deepest selves and subconscious minds, inspiring us to seek a deeper understanding of our existence.*

Truth, OWM

Tell no white lies, cause no others to deceive, say nothing false, let truth be your reprieve.

Follow truth, and truth will hallow, with honesty, all wealth will come to follow.

Truth encompasses non-greed, generosity pure, to accept without gratitude is theft, of that be sure.

Small theft or great, makes no difference here, stealing words or diamonds, both equally severe.

My abundance may cause embarrassment's sting, yet in truth and gratitude, humility may ring.

Do your best, smile till smiles return, be an activist of joy, let other hearts discern.

Plague everyone with joy, a life carefree, in a well-controlled mind, serenities free.

Free of control, anxiety loses its might, desire and possession's tight grip, takes flight.

Accept and give with gratitude, both loss and gain, like a river flowing, not stagnant or vain.

Nature knows our generosity and grants her grace, we gain her confidence creating harmonious space.

In this discipline, don't chase person, place, or thing, soon they'll chase you, like birds on the wing.

Why cry when laughter's due? In joy and truth, a life anew.

Lanka: Chapter 2, section VI

Suffering ends when the belief in judgment ceases. *When identification of self with form, desire, and thought ends, so does ignorance and craving. One's judgment becomes free from blame, realizing interdependence as a universal cause. Even accomplishment and achievement loosen their grip. The world's dreamlike fluidity is seen as created by one's mind.*

Magical Thinking, OWM

Magic seems but nonsense to a mind enslaved, in habits of thought, the world imagined is paved.

Identities formed, constructs held dear, yet in this delusion, unity's unclear.

No evil lies in this habitual thought, only survival's desire, or connection's sought. Separate we seem, building identity's wall, passion, duality, renunciation's call.

To let go of known, embrace indivisible, ego dissolves in unity's principle. No "me" or "mine," no "you" or "yours," just solitude coexistent, a single force.

In silent harmony, our spirits align, united in essence, a seamless design.

Boundless and free, we drift in the stream, together yet separate, like stars in a dream.

In this tranquil space where we both reside, no division or borders, no reason to hide.

Understanding oneness, the mind refrains, judgment ceases, opinion wanes.

Magical thinking, objective view, mechanisms of mind, both false and true.

Form, desire, suffering torn apart, freedom in awareness, a liberated heart.

Realm of synchrony, struggle for the highest good, dance of joy, reality understood

Open heart, focused mind, discerning sight, golden threads in everything, not separate, alight.

Awakened, no rush to nirvana's call, life in peace, without judgment's thrall. Compassionate heart, the magical way, solitude of awareness, knowledge's sway.

Destroy illusion, dualism cease, moment of seeing, sudden awakening's peace. **Magical oneness, growing in all, letting go of outcomes, disappointments fall.**

Enlightenment exists in others' rise, in the light of oneness, we realize.

As we've journeyed through the teachings of *the Lanka*, we've uncovered the wisdom that lies beyond the illusions of ego and duality.

The realization that the ego-soul is a construct of sense-consciousness, and the eternal creator is undifferentiated and non-dual, leads us to a deeper understanding of our true nature.

By letting go of judgments, attachments, and the noise of a restless mind, we may awaken to the reality of our interconnectedness and the oneness of all existence.

This path of self-realization is not about the attainment of external goals but about the inner transformation that comes from recognizing our true self as part of the eternal, living intelligence of all life. **Embracing this wisdom, we may find peace, joy, and the magical thinking that sees the world as a reflection of our own awakened mind.** In this state of non-separation, we live in harmony with the universe, embodying compassion, generosity, and the boundless potential of our true selves.

The Four Key Questions

1. What Do I Want to Be?

This question prompts individuals to reflect on their identity and long-term aspirations. It's about envisioning the person you want to become, encompassing qualities, values, and roles. This introspection is crucial for setting a clear direction in life. For instance, aspiring to be a compassionate leader or a knowledgeable expert in a field guides the choices you make and the skills you develop.

2. What Do I Want to Do?

Focusing on actions and achievements, this question helps clarify goals, hobbies, and personal projects. By identifying what you want to do, you can set specific, actionable goals that lead to fulfilling activities and accomplishments. This question helps in prioritizing efforts and allocating time effectively.

3. What Do I Want to Have?

This question addresses material and non-material desires, such as financial stability, relationships, or a certain lifestyle. It encourages a realistic assessment of needs and desires, aligning them with your values and long-term plans. Understanding what you want to have can drive motivation and provide a tangible benchmark for progress and success.

4. What Am I Willing to Give?

Balancing the previous questions, this focuses on contribution and sacrifice. It emphasizes the importance of reciprocity and the willingness to invest time, effort, and resources for others. This question fosters a sense of responsibility and community, reminding us that achieving our desires involves giving back or supporting others in their journeys.

By regularly revisiting these questions, individuals can maintain clarity and focus, adapt to changing circumstances, and continually evolve towards their envisioned selves.

Thank you very much for sharing my journey! Peace, Love, and Joy!

Made in the USA
Middletown, DE
27 August 2024

59845649R00062